INSIDE THE INSIDE PASSAGE

TRUE STORIES FROM THE LAND OF THE SPIRIT BEAR

CAPTAIN JOSEPH BETTIS

DEDICATION

This book is for my three sons: Dave, Mark and Daniel. Each has his own stories to tell. And for the countless people who guided me along the way.

Contents

CONTENTS

PREFACE

Gabriele Beyer's contributions make the second edition of <u>Inside the Inside Passage</u> a new book. She joined me on *Orina* for three most splendid trips through the Inside Passage and during those times designed the book, drew the maps, produced the pictures and painted the covers. Back from the adventures, she managed the book through the self-publishing process.

The result is a book from both of us. If you want to see more of Gabi's pictures and paintings from the Inside Passage as well as her other magnificent paintings, sculptures, silk paintings, scarves and ties, visit her at www.artbygabriele.com.

Gabi and I chose to self-publish <u>Inside the Inside Passage</u> because we wanted the book to create a more intimate connection between our experiences and the reader. Traveling the Inside Passage is an external challenge and an internal transformation. We wanted to share as much of that experience with you as possible.

Others have also helped make <u>Inside the Inside Passage</u> a better book. Karen Baer read the text and applied her command of English ruthlessly to my sometimes stumbling grammar. Amanda Tarkington also read the entire text and made many valuable contributions. Without the help of Norm Skan in Ketchikan, *Orina* would probably still be there with a dysfunctional anchor winch. Norm, thanks for your professional help and warm friendship.

The acknowledgements for help with the first edition are still appropriate. Sandra Stone constructed the website at www.northwestcaptain.com and provided cover pictures for the first edition. A friend without equal for many years, she also served as crew on some of the adventures. Thank you, Sandra. Visit her beautiful website at www.darkwillowcreek.com.

Brittany Cole Bush e-published the first edition. Thank you, Cole. Meet this remarkable woman at www.brittanhycolebush. com.

Ian and Karen McAllister are heroes. They are naturalists, environmentalists, activists, and parents who walk their talk. Karen and Ian, thank you for many years of friendship and inspiration. See their fantastic work at www.pacificwild.org.

To all the people who live there and who went there with us, and especially to the people of the First Nations who befriended us, thank you. To the other inhabitants of the Inside Passage--the plants and animals of the land, the birds and other critters of the air, the myriad denizens of the deep, the water, rain, wind, and mystery--thank you all.

PREFACE

1 DEPARTURE

*"Aunt Polly allowed how she was going to civilize me. I've
been that route before, so I lit out for the territory."*
                                                    --Huck Finn

The Inside Passage winds a thousand miles through the Pacific Coastal Islands of Washington, British Columbia, and Alaska. From Seattle to Juneau, the route leads past Victoria, Vancouver, Port Hardy, Prince Rupert, Ketchikan, and a dozen other towns and villages. Protected from open ocean by innumerable islands, this classic labyrinth of waterways provides the only access to the world's largest intact temperate rainforest.

Between Seattle and Juneau over 7,000 islands protect the coast, but there are few great beaches or deltas. The Coastal Mountains drop abruptly into the ocean. The great rivers and lesser streams arise in the mountains and flush into the ocean, creating deep inlets which frustrate land travel along the coast. Waterways, therefore, have always provided the only travel paths through the region, serving this function especially well because the islands provide protection from ocean storms.

Ten thousand years ago, and maybe even earlier, when the first humans arrived in the Pacific Northwest, they traveled by canoe. Later, Europeans arrived, not overland but by water. Sailing vessels brought Russian, Spanish, English, and American explorers including the great navigators, Vancouver and Cook. When gold was discovered in the Klondike in 1897, the Inside Passage provided access for thousands of adventurers seeking their fortune in the fabled gold fields of British Columbia and Alaska.

Boats are still the only way through this country, now known as the Great Bear Rainforest. Today the waters are plied by kayaks, native canoes, tug boats, cruise liners, fishermen, loggers, sailors, as well as killer whales, humpback whales, five species of salmon, and myriad other land based and water based creatures.

Though protected from the open ocean, the Inside Passage does have its dangers and challenges. The tides in the region can vary as much as twenty feet from low water to high water. While the tide level rises and falls vertically, vast quantities of water surge horizontally through inlets and passageways seeking ways in and out of the labyrinth. These horizontal tidal currents constitute a major challenge to any mariner. In some constricted passages, the current can reach seventeen or eighteen knots. In 1792, seeing the river-like gush of water through the narrow passage north of Whidbey Island, George Vancouver named the narrow passage Deception Pass.

The Inside Passage is more than a utilitarian highway. Even before the gold rush, the Inside Passage sparked the imagination of those who yearned to escape the definitions of civilization. After the promise of gold had vanished, the Inside Passage continued to inspire fantasies and challenge mariners. Like the South Pacific, the Northwest Passage, and rounding the Horn or the

Cape of Good Hope, the Inside Passage to Alaska evokes a spirit of mystery, the exotic, and adventure. It provides escape from the ordinary and mundane. It challenges the body, mind, and spirit. As clear as the air and the water, its spirit beckons.

Thirty years ago that spirit called me and I headed north. Like most life-path turns, my response to the call of the Inside Passage was not one conscious decision, but serendipitous, the result of numerous small, sometimes unnoticed, unconscious choices. Responding to the call, I found much more than I had expected. There were daunting adventures, rigorous challenges, exotic and surprising pleasures. I found unforgettable people and a wilderness of beauty and fragility beyond imagination.

Previously I was a university professor of philosophy and religious studies. I came to the Pacific Northwest for a new job as a scholar, teacher, and administrator. I stayed as a boat captain and because it seemed like home. I had always been drawn to the wilderness, to the mountains of Colorado and New Hampshire, but far from salt water. At first I continued that pattern in the Northwest—hiking, camping and fishing in the Cascade and Olympic Mountains.

The edge of the ocean was at hand, however, so I bought a boat.

I explored the nearby waters of the San Juan Islands, Gulf Islands, and Desolation Sound. But the call from my restless unconscious would not silence. Each summer I pushed a bit further north, making the ever longer journey in ever larger and better equipped boats, and each summer I learned to appreciate more the challenge and the beauty of this magnificent place. The Inside Passage began to define the rhythm of my life; the academic world receded. For the next three decades the rhythm was set—spring for preparation, summer for the journey, fall to return, winter to rest and plan. My career as an academic and my life as a husband and father had to respond to that rhythm. Sometimes they did and sometimes there was discord. But I could not escape the central melody of water, islands, boats, and people.

Five sturdy boats have carried me through the Inside Passage: *Elsa*, *Raven*, *Sundown*, *Shadow*, and *Loon*. Each appears in the stories that follow. My companions over the years made many and frequently indispensable contributions, adding immeasurably to the joy of the journeys. The stories are all true, but they are not about me or about my companions; they are about the Inside Passage and the adventure and insights that await there.

As I began to write stories about those experiences, I discovered that I am still hooked. My memory for many other things slips, but I can still remember and visualize every anchorage between Seattle and Juneau. Things have changed since the rush to the Klondike, and they have changed since I began to make the journey. As civilization relentlessly encroaches, the wilderness recedes. Nevertheless the adventure and challenge are still there, at least for a little while. My next boat, *Orina*, has arrived.

Seven of the following chapters trace a journey from Seattle to Glacier Bay with anchorages and stories along the way. They do not constitute a cruising guide, but they do provide a rough outline of a way to make the trip. The rest of the chapters are stories about people, places and events that have enriched my experience of the Inside Passage

The Inside Passage is a quixotic, frustrating and seductive environment. That's the way the wilderness is and that's the way I have experienced it. It is not a seamless narrative. Weather changes unexpectedly, regardless of radios, forecasts, and sky gazing. We meet people, share with them, learn from them, and then move on, not knowing where or when they will anchor next. Killer whales appear when we do not expect them, a salmon hits while we are not paying attention. Over it all lingers the spirit of the first inhabitants and we come upon the remains of their fish traps, pictographs, petroglyphs, big houses, burial sites and cedar harvesting in places where we imagine we are the first humans ever to have walked.

Why does the wilderness call to us? It is a voice from outside our mechanized, pre-packaged, commercialized world. Huck Finn heard it and so did those of us who grew up with the Lone Ranger and Roy Rogers. It is the voice of Zorba, of Nietzsche, of Hesse, of Dionysius, of Shiva, and of Raven. Behind all these, it is the voice of our own soul breathing the unquenchable desire to discover and to be liberated.

I hope my stories will evoke that call for you. If you don't have a boat, or can't make the Inside Passage, I hope my stories will spark the spirit of adventure for you wherever you might find it.

The wilderness is there, the hesitation is within.

2 DIESEL AESTHETICS

I wanted to go to Alaska. I'm not sure just why. Partly it was the guy thing: pushing the envelope. "You walk tall after you've been to Alaska in your own boat," a seasoned skipper had told me. Partly it was Huck Finn: I felt over-civilized. And, although I did not realize it at the time, fundamentally it was a search to re-connect with my self. I needed to rediscover the spirit I had lost when I disconnected from nature. The academy, books, talk, security, ego, prestige had taken over. I had cultivated my mind through three graduate degrees, climbed the academic ladder, published esoteric papers, and achieved a tenured professorship. I had neglected my spirit and its roots in mountains and rivers; in earth, water, plants, and animals. I did not walk tall.

As with many life changes it was due to circumstances more than intention. I lived where the Inside Passage begins. I had a boat. All I had to do was cut the dock lines and head out to Huck's "territory."

Already my wife and I had cruised the San Juan Islands between Victoria, Vancouver, and Seattle. We had explored Desolation Sound in British Columbia. About 100 miles north of Vancouver, Desolation Sound offered a grand summer. Cliffs from snow capped mountains dropped directly into the sea, great salmon fishing, clams and oysters on every beach, water calm and warm enough for swimming. It was a paradise. Beyond Desolation Sound lay terra incognita and some of the most treacherous water of the Inside Passage: the Yuculta Rapids. Why go further?

Because, as usual, I wanted to see what was around the next corner.

Our sturdy wooden boat, *Raven*, had been designed by Ed Monk, a legendary Northwest marine architect. She was a full displacement double-ender, intended for cruises in protected waters. But sturdy though she was, she was marginal for the Inside Passage. Her equipment was minimal. The compass, depth sounder and radio were primitive. A few charts were aboard, but not enough, and no radar, no GPS, no automatic pilot. The adequacy of her skipper and crew pretty much matched the electronics. And although my wife voiced sensible reservations, my need to push further prevailed. We double checked all the systems, loaded on spare parts, tools, clothing, food, and fishing gear.

We cast off.

Tidal currents are a major problem on the Inside Passage. The difference between high and low tide can be as large as twenty feet. This vertical rise and fall creates extreme currents as vast quantities of water move through narrow passages between hundreds of islands. Learning to understand these tidal currents is essential to safe travel. We learned as we went. Maybe not the most prudent method, but definitely unforgettable.

We plotted our course on paper charts with parallels and dividers. We checked off each island and navigation aid as we passed. Today, with GPS and electronic chart plotters, these skills are about as useful as telling time with a sundial or making fire by rubbing sticks. But they are still good skills to have. It's fun, and you never know when the electronics will fail.

It was worth the effort. Every day north gets better. The thick green foliage of the Northwest with its Doug Fir, Hemlock, Red and Yellow Cedar, creates a solid wall right to the water line. The lower branches end in a straight horizontal line defined by high tide. Mountain peaks remain snow covered year round. Protected anchorages entice by their solitude, interrupted only by the calls of ravens, wolves and coyotes, and by the splash of salmon and orcas.

We survived the Yuculta Rapids, the Dent Rapids, the Green Rapids, the Wellbore Rapids, and the fearsome chop of Johnston Strait, arriving finally in God's Pocket, a tiny cove with a small but secure dock. Tucked into the east side of Hurst Island and just off Christie Passage, God's Pocket is aptly named. Secure in all weather, it has long been a favorite of small commercial fishing vessels. Because it is unnamed on the charts it is rarely visited by recreational boaters.

Few voyaging destinations beckon without ambiguity, and God's Pocket is no exception. After Johnston Strait, it offers a chance to rest, to catch your breath. But only a short breather because ahead lies Queen Charlotte Strait, the first open water exposed to the swells of the North Pacific. The evening before we intended the crossing, I walked to the end of the dock and looked out to the northwest. Nothing but water. We might just as well be destined for Japan. What I described to my wife as a bit of uncertainty was actually a roiling knot of fear. Not only did I not know where, when, or whether we would reach Calvert Island and Safety Cove (also deceptively named), I also had no idea how to

9

find Pine Island or Egg Island, two small dots of dry land marking the crossing.

It's always a good idea to discuss the next day's float plan with the crew, so I advanced tentatively, "Maybe we should just head back to Desolation Sound. After all, we've already had quite an adventure." My wife's response was instantaneous, unambiguous, and clear: "You've been talking about Alaska until I'm sick of it and you've dragged me this far. We are NOT turning back now." That seemed to settle matters, if not my stomach, so with a decision made, but confidence still hiding, I returned to my walk on the dock.

The patron saint of mariners, whether Santa Maria de Buenos Aires or Quan Yin, did indeed take pity on us that day for also walking the dock were two well-seasoned Alaska fishermen. Time has consumed for me the names of their boats but not the images. I can still picture them clearly. One was a tough little fiberglass stern picker and the other an ancient troller with a pilot house somewhat smaller than a porta potty. And more clearly etched in my memory is the image of the two fishermen: "Roger-Dodger" McLeod and Floyd "Hang-Em-In-Public" Woolsey as they were known throughout the fishing fleet.

Roger Dodger earned his nickname by his inevitable response to radio communication: "roger-dodger," rather than the usual simpler "roger." He was dark and lanky and a bit taciturn. He ran a dozer at the Everett land-fill during the off season and hunted elk in the fall. Floyd Woolsey acquired his "hang-him-in-public" nickname during his tenure as a sergeant in the Seabees. His invariable advice for dealing with negative workers: "Just take the son of a bitch out and hang him in public. Then get on with the work." Floyd was definitely the senior partner in this remarkable partnership. He was, in fact, a warm and gentle person, and proved to be full of encouragement and advice for me. After some dock talk, during which I'm sure I revealed my anxiety about the morrow, Roger and Floyd took us under their wings and offered to let us serve out our sentence in their company. We would run with them to Ketchikan.

At o-dark-thirty the next morning we reluctantly cast off the security of God's Pocket and followed the pale red and green glow of Floyd's running lights out into the black unknown. Roger-Dodger brought up the rear.

We crossed the seeming endless Strait without incident and before noon passed Safety Cove and entered the tangled maze of islands that define British Columbia's North Coast. It was a long, slow trip. Roger-Dodger made six knots in a following sea. We held off monotony with chats on the radio—anything to pass the time. Someone has said that a long boat trip consists of long periods of boredom interrupted by brief moments of stark terror. We discussed the weather, the water, and food. Roger-Dodger had provisioned his summer with meat from an elk he had killed the previous winter. When the seas got a bit choppy he radioed that he would have to go below and tie his elk burgers to the stove with bailing wire while they cooked. I had a vision of him, relinquishing the wheel and with no auto pilot, in his minuscule galley, trying to keep the meat on the stove and the frying pan off the floor.

One day blended into the next. Each morning we got under way before daylight and each evening anchored after dark. Only Hang-'em-in-Public and Roger-Dodger knew where we were, where we were going, and how we were going to get there, but with regard to these specifics they were men of few words.

For me, there was a beauty to this trip that has seldom been equaled. Each day began with something equivalent to the Fourth Movement of Beethoven's Ninth Symphony when, after a long warm-up of the glow-plugs, the main diesel engine fired off. *Raven* came to life. Lights came on, the radio chattered, hot water flowed, coffee perked, bacon fried, the anchor winched up, anchor light off, running lights on, and *Raven* was underway, snuggled in between Floyd and Roger.

Daylight came, dishes were done, boat chores accomplished. Morning coffee. The watch changed. On the CB, discussions of weather, water and elk-burger's frying. Weather reports on the VHF. Lunch. Naps. Some relaxed time as the watch changed again. Afternoon coffee. Three small boats slowly making their way north through the Inside Passage. Evening. Dinner. Dishes. Coffee. Darkness coming on. Running lights on. Finally to anchor. Running lights off, anchor light on. A radio discussion of the day and plans for the morning. Bedtime preparation.

Finally the engine is quieted. Silence happens. Exhausted, we crawl into bed.

Each day, new territory outside, but inside, a routine settles in. And beneath the various activities and chores, always the steady, unwavering throb of the diesel.

Somewhere between the shreds of fog, maybe along about Grenville Channel, an ontological shift occurred. What had begun as a background of quiet, interrupted by the noise of the engine, reversed itself. Now the steady throb of the diesel became the background, the soundscape, the given, and quiet became an unnatural and artificial interruption. The diesel was something we no longer controlled. On our small boat, far from shore and over what might as well have been twenty thousand fathoms of water, the diesel's rhythmic pulse had become the uncaused cause, the creator of our mystery-enshrouded journey, and we were grateful to have been invited along.

Conventional wisdom has it that while diesel engines are practical, the ultimate aesthetic cruising experience is a boat under sail; no sound but the romance of wind in the rigging and the lapping of waves against the hull. To crank up the engine, say the aesthetes, is to destroy the fantasy, the romance, the beauty of full sails in a fair wind.

There is, however, another aesthetic: the aesthetic of the diesel, less ethereal perhaps, but somehow equally beautiful and romantic in its own way. Always there, always providing creative power: heat, light, movement, nourishment. Properly maintained, a diesel engine is safe and reliable. It can be trusted to bring you to port or to anchor again and again, always safely. "Properly maintained" is the operative factor. Check the oil and water every day; change the filters, zincs, belts and impellers every year. Monitor the engine hours, water temperature, oil pressure, exhaust temperature. Learn the basics of diesel mechanics. Confidence and relaxation come with familiarity and experience. Of course there are the unknowns--injectors, fuel pumps, connecting rods, cylinder liners, bearings, seals, cam shafts, valves, valve seats, pistons, rings. We do not have to understand it all. We only have to realize that if we take care of what we do know, every day the diesel starts and runs, providing the fundamental energy that makes everything else happen.

Unconsciously, we became exquisitely sensitive to any variation in the background sound. Harbor-hopping back in the San Juan Islands or Puget Sound, we could pretty much ignore the diesel. Should something seem not quite right, we could check things out when we got to port. But here, far from marinas and mechanics, beyond help, where port is only the next empty anchorage, we became acutely sensitive to the health of the diesel. It is all we had.

Hourly, as regularly as the glass was turned in the old days, we inspected the engine room. As carefully and consistently as the sailor monitors the shifts in the wind, we monitored shifts in the background energy. Was that a momentary drop in RPM's? Or was it just the way I turned my head? Had the oil pressure dropped abnormally, or was that just the usual result of mid-day warmth? Did the same thing happen yesterday? Check the log. We listened. Nothing had changed. All was well. Eventually we learned to relax without losing our awareness.

The state of relaxed awareness became second nature. The steady throb of the diesel morphed into a source of confidence and freedom. Its aesthetics had liberated us from both over-confidence and fear. We had moved into a new state of awareness: a gift of diesel aesthetics. We could relax.

Of course there are no absolutes. Hoses burst. Seals fail. Filters clog. But these are merely the edge of the unknown. They are like the signature irregularity in the pattern of an oriental rug. Underneath it all was the steady throb of the diesel, bringing the boat and its crew to life. We begin to walk tall.

3 GETTING STARTED: SEATTLE TO DESOLATION SOUND

Seattle to Friday Harbor--81 miles
Friday Harbor to Genoa Bay--34 miles
Genoa Bay to Nanaimo--36 miles
Nanaimo to Lund--75 miles
Lund to Eveleigh Anchorage--15 miles

I first went to Alaska twenty years ago. I had met Walt and Millie Woodward the year before in Desolation Sound and they had given me a copy of their book, How to Cruise to Alaska Without Rocking the Boat Too Much. Besides that, and Chapman, I had a few charts, a compass (not compensated), a depth sounder, and a sixteen channel VFH radio. A local fisherman in Squalicum Harbor had drawn the route on my charts.

Things are different now. Now there are several excellent cruising guides to the Inside Passage. Repairs are available at more places along the way, cell phone and radio communications have evolved, and GPS with electronic charting has become standard. Radar is easier to own and use. Nevertheless, the Inside Passage remains an unfulfilled dream for many boaters, and not

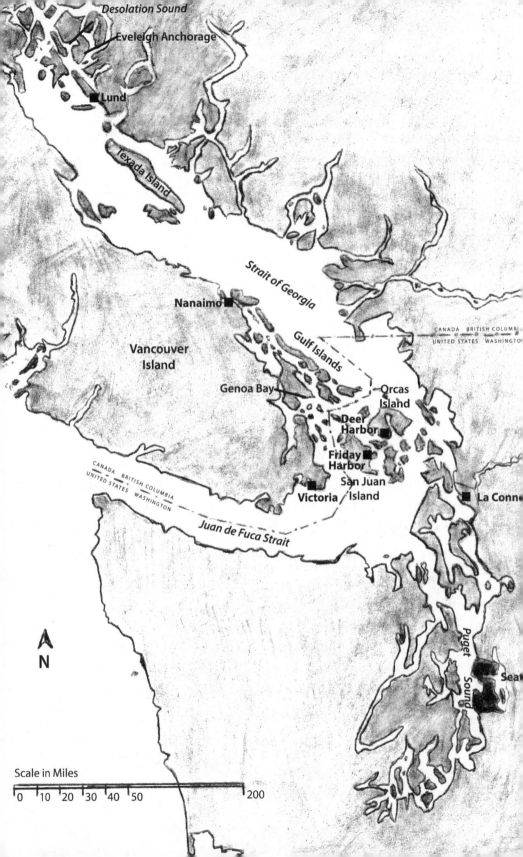

without reason. It is a difficult trip; no doubt about it. Narrows must be carefully negotiated. Several passages of open water are daunting. The weather can be glorious and it can be awful. One summer, it rained every day but six. Why add our folly to Seward's?

Because the rewards are great. It is a magnificent, magical, mysterious, dangerous, safe, maddening, protected waterway. I am fascinated by the intersection of cultures and sub-cultures: First Nations, gillnetters, purse seiners, trollers, sailboats, tug boats, whale watchers, loggers, power boats, kayaks, cruise liners, ferries, sourdoughs, and cheechakos. Each spring I look forward to seeing salmon, orcas, humpbacks, white sides, porpoises, prawns, clams, grizzlies, black bear, moose, elk, deer, wolves, river otters, sea otters, eagles, gulls, osprey. Each fall I remember mountains, glaciers, whirlpools, tidal currents, red tide, northern lights, waterfalls, cascades, hot springs, 16 knot tidal rapids, endless inlets. And always I hold close the quiet anchorages shared only with bears and wolves.

The Inside Passage has been one of the great adventures of my life. Sooner or later, and lately it has become increasingly later than sooner, I cross a demarcating line. It is uncharted, and as imaginary as longitude. At that moment I realize that the animals, sea life, water, islands, and mountains are no longer in my world; I am in their world. The Inside Passage is not just a cruise to Alaska, it is a journey of the spirit. Somehow, I feel free.

All things change. As we humans expand our range, the imaginary line moves further north. I get older. The adventure recedes. Civilization advances. Less frequently do I hear on the VHF, "Morning Cap. Red to red OK with you?"--the distinctive language of tug boat captains passing port to port. There are more boats, more whale watchers, more regulations. The salmon and halibut are harder to catch and there are fewer of them. "Go again," a voice says, "while the imaginary line is still there."

There are other, less imaginary but equally significant lines--spatial "joints"--like an elbow or knee, where the bones and muscles take off in a different direction. The first is the Strait of Georgia, when you leave the relative civilization of Vancouver Island and cross back over to the less accessible mainland. The second "joint" is at the Yuculta Rapids. Here the tides from the Strait of Juan de Fuca and the south end of Vancouver Island meet the tides from Queen Charlotte Sound and the north end of Vancouver Island. Below the Yuculta's the tide floods to the north and ebbs to the south. After the Yuculta's, the tide floods to the south and ebbs to the north. Here the weather, water, trees, and islands all change.

The third "joint" is Queen Charlotte Strait, the first really serious open water crossing. It is the point of no return. Once across, you can reach the comfort of familiar things like automobiles, streets, and stores as easily by continuing north as by retreating south. The final transition is Dixon Entrance, the boundary between British Columbia and Alaska. Once again you are exposed to open water. And once across, the mountains are bigger, the water more open, the anchorages further apart, the shelter of the islands less accessible.

Passing through these spacial zones declares the distance you have come more graphically than passing through time zones flying across the continent.

Time is the key. The fool catcher is out there waiting for the mariner who is late for work back home and cannot sit out a blow. If the weather acts up, be prepared to wait it out. In <u>Exploring</u>

the Inside Passage to Alaska, Don Douglass and Reanne Hemingway-Douglass give an "Ultra Marathon" itinerary of 28 days from Anacortes to Juneau and back, and a "Dream" itinerary of 97 days. I would say skip the marathon and go for the dream. For those without that much time, hire a skipper to take your boat to key destinations and fly in and out. Bella Bella and Sitka would be my choice meeting places. Or make the trip north, fly back if you must, and hire a skipper to bring your boat back. I like to leave as early in the summer as possible, mid May or the first of June. In any event I want to be back across Queen Charlotte Strait before Sept 15.

Books to read: Don Douglass and Reanne Hemingway-Douglass have the most comprehensive cruising guides. For the overall trip there is Exploring the Inside Passage to Alaska. They also have more detailed books on British Columbia and on Alaska. Charlie's Charts North to Alaska by Charles E. Wood is essential if for no other reason than his information about how to transit the Yuculta and other rapids north of Desolation Sound. And, of course, Northwest Boat Travel and Waggoner Cruising Guide.

To nourish the spirit, I bring James Michener's Alaska, Ballard Hadman's As the Sailor Loves the Sea, and John Upton's Alaska Blues.

However all that is ahead. Now we must begin.

I live in the San Juan Islands, but for those who come from further south, Friday Harbor is the last stop before Canada. There are shops, galleries, the Whale Museum, a small shipyard, and stores to buy some of the things you forgot.

In the past, I have most often cleared Canadian Customs at Bedwell Harbour, now called Poet's Cove, on South Pender Island. But this summer I'm going to clear at Van Isle Marina in

Tsehum Harbour and then head for Genoa Bay Cafe for dinner. What I do next depends on the tides at Dodd Narrows. Dodd Narrows, just eight miles south of Nanaimo, must be transited at or near slack water, so I calculate back from there. If my timing is right, I head for Nanaimo. If the tides don't cooperate, I anchor in Montague Harbour and plan for slack at the Narrows the next day. Once through the Narrows, I call ahead for dock space in Nanaimo. After Victoria, Nanaimo is the largest town on Vancouver Island. It used to be a rough and raw fishing village; now it has been gentrified. It is respectable, charming, delightful and not nearly so interesting.

It is traditional to leave Nanaimo at first light, and I believe in tradition. Leaving early, through Newcastle Island Passage, careful to avoid Oregon Rock and Passage Rock, from Departure Bay, it is usually possible to get across the Strait of Georgia before the wind picks up. There have been times when I guessed wrong. Then I found good anchorage about half way across in Bull Passage between Texada and Lasqueti Islands. If the weather is good, I clear the southern tip of Texada and head for Pender Harbour. The passage up Malaspina Strait is dull, so if the weather continues holding, I just keep going. If I can't make it to Lund, there is anchorage around Hardy Island, and moorage at Westview Marina near Powell River.

At one time, Powell River was the largest paper mill in the world. You could always tell when a boat had been in Malaspina Strait because her bow was discolored from the tannin released into the water by the mill. One year I was lucky enough to get to Powell River in time for the world championship paper packing contest. It's not what you think. Main Street was roped off. A flat-bed truck was with various sized rolls of newsprint from the paper mill was parked in the middle of the street. A fork life would place a roll of paper on the backpack of a contestant and he would stagger down the street with his burden. It was an elimination contest. They began with about 200 pounds and each round the weight was increased. Gradually contestants dropped out until in the six hundred pound range, only one gladiator remained. While writing this story, I called the visitor's bureau in Powell River to see if the world championship paper packing contest still happens. "No," she said, "I've never heard of that." This year, she informed me, Powell River is hosting a wine tasting event and an international choral festival. I guess the age of gladiators is over.

If I stop in Powell River now, I visit April White's Wind Spirit Gallery and Jitterbug Café. April was born in Haida Gwaii, formerly the Queen Charlotte Islands, and through her father is a member of the Eagle Clan and a direct descendant to the renowned Haida artist Charles Edenshaw. Her work and other artists represented in her gallery can be seen at www.windspirit.com.

Lund is the last town until Port McNeill. There is a small store, a repair facility and a good restaurant. From Lund, it's just around the corner to Desolation Sound. After the Fourth of July the anchorages in Desolation Sound are crowded. Earlier in the season, however, there are many uniquely beautiful and well protected retreats. The water, especially in Pendrell Sound, is warm enough for swimming, and if there is no red tide alert, the oysters are some of the best in the world.

The Yuculta Rapids are next, so a lay day or two in Desolation Sound is always a good idea.

4 If The Boat's Not Sinking, It Isn't A Crisis

After my first trip to Alaska, I knew I had to go back. And I knew to return I had to have a bigger boat. In boating, one thing follows another. The only way I could afford a bigger boat was to sell the house. That meant living aboard. That meant a much bigger boat. So the search began.

With *Sundown*, it was love at first sight--at least for me. My wife had reservations. Very big boat. Very big dirty boat. (Why is every boat we buy dirty and broken while every boat we sell is clean and works?) Very needy big dirty boat: Needs paint. Needs electrical work. Furnace doesn't work. Refrigerator doesn't work. Kitchen stove, aka galley range, doesn't work. Water coming out of the taps looks funny and tastes worse. Auto pilot doesn't work.

These, however, are minor blips on the radar (doesn't work) when true love is afoot. Walt Masland, the proud and capable skipper of Pelican, who taught me more than I can ever properly thank him for, said, "In boats, function follows form. If she's not graceful she won't sail properly." *Sundown* was graceful.

Built in 1924 at the famous Menchion's Yard near Vancouver, B.C., *Sundown* was intended as a packer for Nel-Bro, the large

25

Canadian fishery company. She was to haul fish from the fleet on the west side of Vancouver Island to processing plants on the mainland. Three years later she was rebuilt at Benson's shipyard and sold to Mac and Mac Hardware Company, which owned a large hardware store in Victoria. The store, now Victoria Iron and Steel, is still there in Victoria, just up the street from the Empress, but no longer sells old boating junk in the basement as they did back when *Sundown* worked for them

Back then, Mac and Mac loaded *Sundown* up with hardware and catalogs and sent her around Vancouver Island, peddling their wares. Capt. Bowles skippered her for thirty years, and part of her mission was to take managers from remote logging and fishing operations out for a cruise, salmon fishing, food and drink. Then, large orders for hardware were sometimes discussed. It is only speculation that the size of the order depended on the size of the catch and the depth of the bottle. But that's another story.

I was in love with *Sundown*. We could barely afford her if we sold the house. She was big enough to live aboard. There was even a full size bathtub. That the hot water heater didn't work was just another of those minor irritations.

A more serious irritation was the fact that I hadn't a clue about what I was doing. It didn't matter that the radar didn't work because I didn't know how to use it anyway. Although I managed to effectively suppress my wife's reservations, as well as my own, anxiety remained and increased as I faced the complexity of things. The engine room was a maze of wires, pipes, hoses, and mysterious mechanical objects. There were no clues about which of them worked and which didn't nor about their function if they did work. The engine seemed to be about the size of a locomotive, with a significant number of unidentifiable accessories.

My community college course in diesel mechanics was obviously inadequate. This was graduate school, and I had a steep learning curve ahead. Up on top, the "boat deck" I was instructed, there were winches, davits, pulleys (blocks), a dubious looking skiff with an ancient outboard, and outriggers for large triangular things called paravanes, whatever that meant. The ground tackle consisted of threes: a three-hundred pound navy anchor, three hundred feet of 9/16 steel cable and an anchor winch with a drum about three feet in diameter. The winch was operated by the main engine through a series of roller chains and jack shafts, just like my old Schwinn bike. Well, almost.

Nevertheless, we proceeded to survey. On land, *Sundown* looked twice the size. The expanse of red bottom paint seemed about the size of a basket-ball court. I got a crick in my neck looking up. But the magic of love continued and grew as I watched the skill of the shipwright as he replaced 2x6x16 planks, and caulked their seams. The magic only slightly dimmed when I learned the rule of thumb: "It takes one shipwright and one assistant one day to replace one plank and costs one thousand dollars." Later I would learn to substitute "boat unit" for "one thousand dollars." It's shorter, and hides some of the misery.

The survey also exposed some additional minor irritations. Since I didn't fully understand what it meant that the ends of several planks showed signs of dry-rot, it really didn't sink in.

The moment of decision arrived. *Sundown* had been surveyed. To say she "passed survey" would be spin. We had the financing. We could make the payments if, as my wife inconveniently reminded me, we sold the house. We had survived the sea trials. My wife was, to put it mildly, not ecstatic, but at least resigned. The decision was mine. This was not only buying a dirty and largely broken tangle of machinery and wood called a "boat," it was committing to a radically new lifestyle: living aboard. The moment had arrived and the life-changing decision could no longer be delayed or avoided. It was time to fish or cut bait.

It was the evening after the survey. We were in the saloon and I was sweating out the decision, the pros and cons. Would my wife jump ship, stuff like that. One of the bright spots in this sad tale of young boat love was the surveyor. Lee Earheart was one of the very best in the Northwest and undoubtedly he had seen this scene play out many times. Lee was sitting in the wicker chair in the saloon doing something strange with a sack of what looked like the remains of dreadlocks in a barber shop. He explained that it was oakum, a mixture of tar and jute, used to caulk the seams. Not normally sold at West Marine, nor of much use in fiberglass boats. He was preparing it for the next day's work of plugging the leaks in *Sundown*. Just another minor irritation.

The tension of the love affair was growing. On the one side was my heart, on the other, all these minor irritations. My wife was strangely quiet.

Finally, Lee looked up. "Joseph," he said, "Remember, if the boat's not sinking it isn't a crisis." And my fate was sealed. *Sundown* was bought, the seams were caulked, the house sold, and we were off to Alaska.

I suppose you could say my love affair was consummated. At least you could say that for the next ten years, *Sundown* occupied most of my energy, time, and affection. If *Sundown* ever had a competitor for my affection, it was not another boat. It was the journey--The Inside Passage. (My wife, meanwhile, had jumped ship.)

Fred C. Clark, who cruised Northwest waters for many years

aboard *Kay II* and introduced me to a few of the arcane and use-less rituals of "yachting," had said, "After you've been to Alaska, you walk tall." And there is some truth there. It is an accomplish-ment. But traveling the Inside Passage is not only about Alaska. It is not a destination cruise. It is not like going to the moon, I assume, where the passage is merely an inconvenient necessity of reaching the objective. The Inside Passage is the objective. This is not about "boating" or "yachting" or a rendezvous of old dock buddies. It is about the legendary Northwest and the magic of the Inside Passage.

It is about freedom. Edward Abbey got it right in <u>Desert Solitaire</u>.

"Do not burn yourselves out. Be as I am--a reluctant enthusi-ast--a part-time crusader, a half-hearted fanatic. Save the other half of yourselves and your lives for pleasure and adventure. It is not enough to fight for the land; it is even more important to enjoy it. While you can. While it's still there. So get out there and hunt and fish and mess around with your friends, ramble out yonder and explore the forests, encounter the grizzly, climb the mountains, bag the peaks, run the rivers, breathe deep of that yet sweet and lucid air, sit quietly for a while and contemplate the precious stillness, that lovely, mysterious and awesome space.

Enjoy yourselves, keep your brain in your head and your head firmly attached to the body, the body active and alive, and I promise you this much: I promise you this one sweet victory over our enemies, over those desk-bound people with their hearts in a safe deposit box and their eyes hypnotized by desk calculators. I promise you this: you will outlive the bastards."

And remember: If the boat's not sinking, it isn't a crisis. I have never regretted the decision.

5 Raven And The Three Fat Boys

Around boats, one thing always seems to follow another. Karma flourishes in a marine environment. So, if you ever need empirical confirmation of the Buddhist teaching about interdependence, just hang out around boats for a while. It works both ways: if you pay attention, prepare well, take care of maintenance, and practice prudent boating, the trip will in all likelihood be wonderful. But if your attention wavers, the fool catcher will be waiting as he was for *Raven* and the three fat boys.

I had a feeling the doorway to the downward path opened when I sold *Raven* to Jim and his two partners. But they paid cash, and my heart had already been captured by my new love, *Sundown*, so I became an accomplice before the fact and karma took it from there. I had taken great good care of *Raven*, and she was in excellent condition for her new owners. Her paint was sound and bright, all systems were working and there were ample spare parts and fittings. I went over the boat with Jim--deck plates for water and fuel, extra parts, spare alternator, starter, solenoid, all carefully wrapped and sealed. We reviewed fuses, gaskets, impellers, bilge pumps, engine alarms, high bilge water alarms, paint locker, life vests, and all the rest. But my mitigation efforts were to no avail; Jim was practically peeing in his pants in his eagerness to get out on the water.

Jim's two business partners were also partners in the boat, and between the three of them they probably weighed somewhere between 750 and 800 pounds, a fact that will take on significance later in the story. But *Raven's* maiden voyage under new owner-ship was reserved for Jim, his wife, and their daughter. In hasty and pretentious preparation to escape the mainland, Jim filled the water tanks with diesel and topped off the fuel tank with water. Since there was still a good slug of fuel in the lines and fil-ters, they were able to get well into the islands before the engine quit.

Since I had put new batteries in *Raven* before I sold her, their repeated efforts to start the engine burned up the starter before the batteries ran down. Eventually they were able to get a tow into Friday Harbor.

It was Fourth of July Weekend. The marina was packed and tourists were streaming off the ferries on bicycles and motor-cycles, in cars, SUVs, campers, and fifth wheelers. Hoards were afoot. The heat was intense and oppressive, and the local chan-dleries and marine mechanics were having a field day. Adding to the misery, the water on the boat tasted awful and a shower was even worse, so Jim's wife and daughter took a float plane home. Forgetfulness being a concomitant of mindlessness, Jim forgot the spare starter tucked safely away but finally found a mechanic who would rewind the failed one--$400. Cleaning the water and fuel tanks proved even more costly. But eventually, late for work, several hundred dollars poorer, hot and unhappy, Jim returned to Bellingham from *Raven's* maiden voyage.

The next trip was reserved for the partners: a major fishing expedition. The fish weren't hitting that day, but the sun and beer were good, and the water was fine and the boat ran well--until it quit. Evidently the mechanic had not bled all the water from the fuel tank and lines. This time the batteries ran down before the starter burned up.

But the fat boys were resourceful. This was not a wimpy family outing. They put the dingy in the water, attached a line to *Raven*, and one of the partners commenced to row the ship back to Bellingham. The other two sat on the sun deck and worked on the beer.

Somewhere near Chuckanut Bay someone noticed that the shoreline was moving in the direction the boat was supposed to be moving. That could mean only one thing. The current taking them away from home was stronger than the rowing pulling them toward home. So they called the third man back to finish the beer and to hold a partnership conference.

Now the size of the three guys becomes a factor. There was a dandy ladder on *Raven* to aid movement from ship to dingy and back, but the third fat boy was exhausted from the rowing and couldn't make it up and into the cockpit. So his two friends came down to help. Still, it was a struggle. So he stood on the gunnels of the dingy to gain a little additional height.

The dingy turned over, filled with water, and sank. The fat boy followed the dingy into the salt chuck. But his partners were holding on. One also held the painter to the descending dingy, which was more of a problem than a solution since it interfered with recovery of the man overboard. So, after receiving explicit and unequivocal instructions about what to do with the rope, he let the dingy sink and turned to help pull the partner aboard.

33

Finally, they were successful. All three were safe and secure in *Raven's* cockpit and all 750-800 pounds of them on the same side of the cockpit. The deck gave way. But it didn't give way completely. The engine was under the cockpit and the manifold and exhaust pipe held the deck mostly up.

Eventually they were able to get a tow back to Bellingham.

A week later, with a new dingy and oars and a new bill for cleaning the fuel tank, the partners went fishing again. Unfortunately, however, while the engine manifold had prevented a complete collapse of the deck earlier, the weight of the fat boys had cracked the manifold. The exhaust, instead of leaving through the exhaust pipe, was now dumping into the engine compartment and the compartment caught on fire. Fortunately, they were able to put out the fire and get a tow back to Bellingham.

After the burned wiring in engine compartment had been replaced, *Raven's* fourth voyage under new ownership was a solo trip by a friend of the family. Evidently he had a delightful cruise and returned safely to the harbor without a tow, but when he stepped down from the steering station, he found he was standing above his ankles in water. He was still in the main cabin. The automatic bilge pump wasn't working.

The fool catcher sometimes has a macabre sense of humor: I happened to be on the dock when *Raven* and the friend returned. Evidently, although I was no longer her owner, I had not yet escaped *Raven's* karmic wheel. I showed the friend how to work the manual bilge pump, brought my emergency pump from *Sundown*, and we got most of the water out.

Then I began to look for the problem. The bilge pump had overheated and blown its fuse. The friend said that the bilge pump had run continually during the first part of his cruise, but when it finally quit he enjoyed the quiet, and forgot about it.

What had happened? Water in the fuel tank had caused the engine to die. Cranking the engine had burned out the starter and run down the batteries. Unable to restart the engine, the three partners had tried to row the boat home. When that didn't work, they sank the dingy and their collective weight broke the deck over the engine compartment. The broken deck cracked the manifold which caused the engine to dump both hot exhaust and cooling water into the engine compartment. The hot exhaust started a fire and the cooling water flooded the boat. The strain on the bilge pump caused it to overheat and blow a fuse.

Raven now seems to be permanently moored at the dock. The dock lines are a bit moldy, the stack of empty beer cans in the dock box grows, and the paint peels. Visible through the partly open curtains, an unfinished poker game is spread on the dinette table. The karmic wheel turns. Around boats one thing always seems to follow another.

6 Buddy

Before all the salmon had been caught, and before *Sundown* arrived, each year I took *Raven* to Stuart Island in British Columbia to fish. Stuart Island was a hot spot and people came from everywhere to fish that special place. John Wayne brought his boat, *Wild Goose*, which he docked at Big Bay Marina. Then, like the rest of us, he fished from a small skiff for the wonderful, wild, Chinook salmon.

Stuart Island lies at the mouth of Bute Inlet, one of the largest fjords on the Inside Passage. Bute reaches back thirty-eight miles into the core of the Canadian Coastal Range where it is fed by the Homathko Snowfield and by the Southgate River. For most of its thirty-eight miles, the inlet is two miles wide and two thousand feet deep. As the tides enter and leave the inlet twice each day, over one hundred and fifty billion gallons of water surge around Stuart Island through the Arran and Yuculta Rapids. These intense currents create a maelstrom of whirlpools, overfalls and turbulence. Twice daily the normally tranquil Inside Passage becomes a raging white-water river. This is truly dangerous water; boats headed both north and south wait for slack tide before passing. There is never really a slack calm, but the currents do wane as the tide turns. Then they begin again, this time in the opposite direction.

The churning water is rich in oxygen, and the oxygen encourages the growth of phytoplankton. The phytoplankton soup attracts zooplankton and the zooplankton attract krill. The krill attract herring; the herring attract salmon; and the salmon attract eagles and fishermen.

During the evening bite, there were frequently fifty small boats trolling through the schools of salmon and below the circling eagles. Continually you would hear "fish on," or see a fisherman in a nearby boat set the hook as his seven-foot salmon rod dipped into the water. It was fascinating to watch the guides handle inexperienced fishermen by giving them very limber rods and setting the drag of their reel loose, so they would not lose the fish. These tactics also insured that it would take a long time to land the fish and attract attention from people in other boats. It was like the practice in a casino letting the jackpot bell ring for a long time before the attendant arrives. But, most of all, it was a wonderful time of camaraderie, with plenty of fish for everyone.

As the bite ended and it became too dark to fish, the boats made their way back to Big Bay or to the small dock at Stuart Island. In *Raven* we returned through a narrow passage between Sonora and Maurelle Islands, a passage called "Hole-in-the-Wall," to anchor for the night in Florence Cove. After dinner we would tend to the beautiful, silver, iridescent salmon, carefully cleaning and icing them, or canning them in pint jars to take home for the winter.

Florence Cove was a tricky anchorage with poor holding ground, but it was the only one nearby, and the docks at the marinas and fishing resorts were crowded and noisy. I remember one night when it blew pretty hard, our anchor drug. My son, Mark, woke me, and we watched as *Raven* was blown relentlessly toward the rocks. *Raven's* engine was a German-made MWM. To start the engine, you had to heat glow-plugs. Precious minutes ticked by as I waited for the starting temperature. Finally, the engine fired and we pulled away. In pouring rain and black darkness, Mark went to the foredeck to reset the anchor and my heart rate started to settle down.

The next day we spent several hours learning more about Florence Cove. Cruising back and forth, watching the fathometer, we got some idea of the contours of the bottom. And with repeated trials at anchoring, we found ground that would hold. For several years after that wet night, we anchored comfortably, realizing we would be safely tucked inside the easterly entrance to the Cove.

One evening when we rounded that easterly point, and entered Florence Cove, hungry and ready for solitude, instead we found a float house! It was a cabin, built on a raft of logs, anchored in the best location, "our" spot. From the raft a narrow log walkway led ashore.

We chose another anchorage further from the point, more exposed, but probably safe, given predictions of good weather.

After dinner I saw a man fishing from the float cabin. Wondering who the hell had staked out their house in "our" anchorage, I put our skiff in the water and rowed in his direction. Well, not exactly in his direction. In those days and places, etiquette dictated that one approach a stranger obliquely, rowing on a tangent to the target and giving the other person ample opportunity to recognize the invited meeting and wave you over, or look away. The fisherman waved me over and that was the beginning of a beautiful friendship that lasted until Buddy died of lung cancer fifteen years later.

Buddy was an Indian. Now I know that's politically incorrect. Well, it's not politically incorrect to be an Indian, but to call someone that. Buddy belonged to the First Nations. But to me, he looked like an Indian. Or at least he looked like what I thought an Indian should look like. He was bare-chested, his hair was long and black, and his face was as rough and craggy as Richard Boone's Paladin.

As we got to know each other over the years, I learned that Buddy had grown up as an outcast. His band was too small to have survived the 1863 smallpox genocide. Without governmental recognition as a person, he drifted in and out of an alien society. During earlier years he worked as a bouncer at a strip club. He shot up heroin. He drank whatever was cheap and available. He fought. He went to prison. Then somehow, something changed. Buddy realized that fighting was not the answer. By the time I met him he was a very gentle man. He was a painter and a poet, and we became friends.

But that evening he was just a guy fishing from a cabin on a raft of logs where I wanted to anchor. "How's the fishing?" The usual opener. "Not too bad." The usual reply. I let the skiff drift closer. Buddy reached down to steady it against the log, definitely a friendly act. After a protracted ritual conversation about boats, fishing and weather, Buddy invited me to tie *Raven* at the float cabin. After that when the evening bite ended, we no longer had to search for anchorage. We had our own private, quiet, safe dock .

The float cabin belonged to Wayne and Charlene. Wayne was a cod fisherman and Buddy and Susie were crew on his boat, the *Jan Elaine*. During the fishing season Buddy and Susie lived with

Wayne and Charlene and their two-year-old son, Charlie, in the float cabin. Wayne and Charlene were proud that they had never paid rent or mortgage. They had salvaged logs from the beaches, tied them together with cables abandoned by loggers, and built the cabin with mostly scrounged lumber. There was a small fresh-water stream that emptied on the shore behind the float and ample wood for heat and cooking on the beach and in the woods. Florence Cove provided fish, clams, oysters, prawns, and wild green plants. They were pretty well set up.

I never knew if Buddy and Susie were married. It just didn't seem important. As long as I knew them they were a dedicated and devoted couple. The three of us had some dandy times together. As I left Jervis Inlet one fall, Susie gave me a small Tsimshian carving, "Mystical Warrior." On the back, barely legible, in ball point pen: "Mystical Warrior holding Haida Chief's talking stick, carved by Peter Charlie Capilano Reservation Squamish Band V.I.B.C." Later I gave Susie a gold Raven ring magnificently carved by Francis Williams, a Vancouver artist. Buddy gave us his wisdom, his vision, his drawings, and his poetry.

Days with Buddy were filled with stories and adventures, and although he infrequently left Jervis Inlet, he was wise, gentle, and very much loved. When he died, the ceremony and celebration for his life was attended by over two hundred people. They all came to Jervis Inlet by boat or sea plane.

Although Buddy and Susie were poor by most standards, their lives were rich. When it became known that Buddy was dying, a wealthy friend invited them to live in his magnificent waterfront home. The house was on a small cove, hidden and protected by forbidding rock cliffs. I could not see the narrow entrance, but on the radio Susie assured me that she could see me and I was on course. And just before I was on the rocks, I saw the channel. It was a narrow entrance into a small, quiet little lagoon, a magical spot. There was a small dock and enough room for *Sundown* and one other boat. In that almost invisible little paradise were stables and a horse, gardens, and a magnificent timber frame home on pilings at the tide line.

Buddy was obviously very sick, visibly worse than when I had seen him a couple of weeks earlier in a Vancouver hospital. But he was sitting up and still Buddy--quiet, poetic, philosophical, and visionary. The gleam and distance that had always been in his eyes continued to draw me to him. We talked quietly for a long afternoon. As his pain increased, Susie managed his meds; marijuana, morphine, and heroin allowing him to remain hovering somewhere between pain and ease, between clarity and sleep. I slept on *Sundown* that night and left after breakfast the next morning. Buddy died two weeks later.

A couple of years later, Susie took up with Paul, a fisherman who had been a friend for many years. One afternoon as they were crossing Jervis Inlet in a cold rain and rough sea, the fool catcher got Susie. When Paul realized she had fallen overboard, he retraced his route. Friends say that he found her, grabbed her hand, but in the cold rain and rough sea, could not hold on. It was some of the deepest water in the Inlet--over a thousand feet.

Although I do not know for sure, I believe Susie was wearing the Raven ring on a chain around her neck. "Mystical Warrior" hangs on the wall to the left of my desk. It's a beautiful small piece of Northwest art, but beyond that, it calls me to the space and time I shared with Buddy and Susie.

I never went back to Jervis Inlet after Buddy and Susie died, and after the salmon were gone, I no longer visited Stuart Island.

But once, I returned to Florence Cove. I wanted to see again the quiet, remote little anchorage where good clams could be dug at low tide and rock cod caught from the boat, and where I met Buddy and Susie. This time, rounding the point, anticipating a return to that past and secure wilderness, and remembering the float house and Buddy, Susie, Wayne, Charlene, Charlie, and the *Jan Elaine*, we were met by a landscape scraped and torn to raw, red dirt. The hills of Maurelle Island were stripped bare, right down to the rocks and beaches of the tidelands.

"Clear cutting" is an oxymoron. There is nothing clear about it. It is ugly and brutal and destroys a fragile beauty created over hundreds of years. The yarders and dozers were still at work higher up, and the growling of their engines and crash of their destruction reverberated across the water. Although the noise was deafening and the destruction beyond depressing, it was almost evening and we anchored in the old spot. Later, when the loggers loaded into their fast crew boats to return to Harriot Bay for the night, with the cove finally silent, we talked about Edward Abbey and his monkey wrench gang.

We left early the next morning, hoping to forget what we had seen and heard, and hoping to remember instead those few years while there were still salmon to catch, and when, after the evening bite, we returned to safe anchorage in Florence Cove and to Buddy's welcoming grin.

7 THROUGH THE YUCULTAS: DESOLATION SOUND TO ALERT BAY

Lund to Eveleigh Anchorage--15 miles
Eveleigh Anchorage to the Yucultas--27 miles
The Yucultas to Forward Harbour--28 miles
Forward Harbour to Alert Bay--48 miles

Before I went to Alaska, Desolation Sound was our yearly destination. Things were not so crowded then, and the fishing was good. Stuart Island was one of the great salmon fishing areas of the Northwest. Besides the Chinook and Coho salmon, there were Golden Eye Rock Fish, which we called red snapper, ling cod, and plenty of clams, oysters, prawns, and mussels. We did not have to worry about pollution or red tide

I found a small bight, inside Pendrell Sound, that was barely big enough for *Raven*. I dropped the anchor outside the large, covered rock in the middle of the entrance and backed in over it. Then I ran two stern lines ashore, and I was home. As the tide rose the shore lines became slack, but the anchor rode kept us in place. And when the tide ebbed there were oysters on the beach. When we ran out of water or gin, it was a short trip to Refuge Cove

and back again. I tied strings around the trees I used for the shore lines, and returned to them year after year. The water was warm enough for swimming

In those days, Lund was the last stop before Desolation Sound and the first stop on the way south. I'm not sure why I was so attracted to that north country, but I was. Each Spring, when I crossed Georgia Strait and left the civilization of Vancouver Island I felt free. I felt that I was returning to the best part of my life. And each autumn when I stopped at Lund, I felt like that part of my life was over for another year and I was headed back. I started to say "headed home", but I think home was always north. I was just headed back.

That last night in Lund was a ritual, a wake, a farewell celebration and ceremony. By that time, we were out of gin again, but there was a store in Lund. We would stop in the Ragged Islands for oysters. On the charts these islands are called the Copeland Islands, and now they are a marine park. Now it is probably illegal to pick oysters there. Or they have been all picked over. Or they are polluted. I liked it better when they were known as the Ragged Islands, when they were not a marine park, and when the oysters were clear and clean and firm.

Lots of oysters, both wild and farmed, grow in Desolation Sound because the water is warm, but I think some of the best were in the Raggeds because the water was cold and clear and flushed twice a day with the tide. With our sack of oysters, we would head for Lund. There we would buy ice, gin, tonic, lemons, limes, and horseradish. We put the oysters on the grill until they popped, and ate them with horseradish and lemon, and drank the gin with tonic and limes. The combination was, well, intoxicating

The poignancy of that last night before returning was heightened by the spectacular sunsets in Lund. They seemed more vivid than anywhere else. Their beauty was only slightly diminished when we learned they were produced by the air pollution from the paper mill in Powell River.

Desolation Sound was as far north as we went for several years. The fishing was excellent, clams and oysters were abundant, the water was warm, and there were many beautiful and peaceful anchorages. Why go further? Desolation Sound was also a good place to turn around because the next day north led through the Yuculta Rapids.

However long you decide to stay in Desolation Sound, if you are still headed north, the next leg of the Inside Passage is determined by the Yuculta Rapids, locally called the Yucklataws, and sometimes just the Yucks. Actually, there is a series of rapids: Yucultas, Dent, Green, and Whirlpool. If you time things right, you can get through all of them and spend the night in Blind Channel or Forward Harbour. But if you don't time things right, it can be one of those boating experiences you would rather not have. One year, I did it wrong, and the whirlpool at Devil's Punchbowl carried *Sundown*, 64 feet and 81 tons, in a 360 degree circle before spitting her out. Now, I just get out my old copy of <u>Charlie's Charts</u>, re-read his instructions, double check the tide tables, and do it the way he says.

During the first years, when the boat was our 26 foot Calkins Bartender, *Elsa*, or the 31 foot Monk-designed *Raven*, after the Yucultas, we would stop at Blind Channel. Almost always there was freshly baked bread and fresh greens from the Garden. The Richter's were warm and hospitable hosts. Over the years Blind Channel has been transformed--gentrified. Now there is internet wireless, a first-class restaurant, and all the amenities boaters seem to want. Their website is worth a good visit, especially its page on the history of Blind Channel.

Blind Channel is blessed and cursed by strong currents at the docks. This made it a difficult stop for *Sundown*, so in those later years we usually passed Blind Channel and headed for anchorage at Forward Harbour. Wellbore Channel separates the mainland from the islands, and we frequently saw black bear there. Forward Harbour is a large and protected anchorage. Sometimes there is a restaurant there, and frequently black bears on the shore. The short walk across the narrow neck to Bessborough Bay provides some good beach combing, but sometimes the presence of a mama black bear and her two cubs made staying on board more appealing.

After Forward Harbour, it's a long slog up Johnston Strait to Alert Bay, Port McNeill and the Broughton Archipelago. The northern terminus of Johnston Strait marks one of the great transition zones of the Inside Passage. It is an area rich in history, First Nations culture, abundant wildlife, good fishing, resources for supplies and repairs, and quiet, remote anchorages. Vancouver Island is 285 miles long and is the world's 42nd largest island, but north of Johnston Strait, Vancouver Island no longer provides protection from the open ocean. Ahead lies Queen Charlotte Strait, open to the Pacific swells that seem to arrive from Japan. It is sixty-five miles to the protection of Pruth Anchorage.

Some people call the Broughton Archipelago "the new Desolation Sound." After their mysterious two or four year's voyage through the far reaches of the Pacific, all of the salmon: Chinook, Coho, Chum, Sockeye and Pink, enter these southern waters around the great Island's northern tip. They make their way into the giant inlets of British Columbia, finding not only the exact stream, but the exact spawning area where they were hatched. The northern resident pods of orca whales spend their summers here, feeding on the salmon and rubbing their bellies on the pebbles in Robson Bight. At least that was the way it was before the fish farms came. Now the sea lice and bacteria introduced by the Norwegian-owned fish farms threaten the entire food chain. And the farmed, artificially colored farmed Atlantic salmon threaten our sense of taste.

When I first visited Telegraph Cove, near the northern end of Johnston Strait, I was looking for Marvin Farrant who, I had been told, knew something of the history of my boat, *Sundown*. Not only did Marvin have a lot of information, he took me into a warehouse there on a pier and showed me a huge three cylinder Atlas diesel, rusting away. "That," he said, "was *Sundown's* first engine. When it was replaced with a more modern engine, the Atlas was put ashore here and it ran the light plant in Telegraph Cove for years. Eventually one of the connecting rods developed a flat on the crankshaft. We took the engine apart and tried to file down the shaft by hand, but it didn't work. So we just disconnected that cylinder and ran her on two for several more years."

Telegraph Cove has changed since then. The developers have arrived. *Sundown's* old rusty Atlas has a new coat of green paint, her brass has been polished and she sits as a center piece of a modern restaurant. Developers have laid out a subdivision, dug a new harbor, and built a large motel. So now I visit Telegraph Cove to see my friends Jim and Mary Bowerman who host unique whale watching cruises aboard their classic Northwest boat, *Gikumi*. They also maintain a fascinating wildlife museum. After Telegraph Cove I head for Port McNeill to visit with Bill and Donna Mackay. Their boat, *Naiad Explorer*, offers great whale watching. The last time I visited Bill and Donna they had almost unbelievable underwater videos of orca whales, standing vertically underwater and riding in the wake of their boat

The Broughtons are home to some of the great bands of the First Nations, including the Kwakwaka'wakw, known for their breathtaking art and mythology. Each year I return to Alert Bay for here is told most vividly the story of genocide and survival of the magnificent indigenous culture of the Kwakwaka'wakw people. Failing to grasp this story is to fail to understand and appreciate the vibrancy of the great Northwest coast.

In 1863, faced with growing hostility as European settlers encroached on First Nations land, the colonial government invited representatives from villages between Knight Inlet and Prince Rupert to Victoria ostensibly to settle land claims issues. The indigenous representatives set up camps on the outskirts of town. Over the next weeks, residents from Victoria brought blankets infected with smallpox to the encampment. When the infection had spread throughout the First Nations delegates, the government forced them, with bayonets and guns, to return to their villages, carrying the disease with them. Seventy-five percent of the First Nations people who lived between Victoria and Prince Rupert died. In some villages the virulent disease, against which the First Nations people had no natural antibodies, killed everyone. Those who did survive were left with a monumental struggle to preserve their life and culture in the face of intense pressure from the colonialists. Although there were individuals among the residents of Victoria who viewed these developments with alarm and rendered what help they could, it is still not widely acknowledged that the genocide was intentional. After one hundred and fifty years, the British Columbia government still has not settled land claims issues.

The potlatch was at the center of Kwakwaka'wakw spiritual and cultural life, and in 1864 the colonial government, in its effort to obliterate the remains of the indigenous culture, outlawed it. This ban remained in effect until 1951.

In 1921, in defiance of the ban, Dan Cranmer hosted a great potlatch on nearby Village Island. In retaliation, the government arrested several dozen people and threatened to hold them and arrest more unless the ancient ceremonial regalia was brought to Alert Bay. The native people felt they had no choice. The Indian Agent, William Halliday, and the arresting officer, RCMP Sergeant Donald Angerman, sold some of the artifacts and sent others to museums in Victoria, Ottawa, and Toronto. The rest they burned. Fifty years later, in the 1970's, the Kwakwaka'wakw gained the return of these precious objects and built the U'Mista Cultural Center in Alert Bay and a museum at Cape Mudge to house them. The U'Mista Center not only tells this story of genocide and survival, but stands as a living symbol of the continued survival and growing strength of First Nations culture. Nearby, an abandoned government school witnesses another chapter in the same sad story of struggle and survival.

The U'Mista Center contains a gift shop, a small gallery where an orientation video is shown, and a diorama of photographs from the history of First Nations people in that area. As you enter the main room, the "Potlatch Collection Gallery," there is a small sign: "We had thought about enclosing these precious objects in showcases, but we felt they had been in prison too long. Please be careful." Then you are in the replica of a Big House, and in the midst of ceremonial regalia that defies museum categories. For me, each year, it is a genuinely numinous experience. I just sit for a while, letting it soak in how close this tragic history remains to the living present.

Some years I have been content to spend the entire summer in the Broughtons. The area is rich in myriad ways: Paul and Helena Spong's OrcaLab, Kingcome Inlet's pictographs, Hansen Island's culturally modified trees, Max and Anca's Kwatsi Bay, Alexandra Morton, Billy Proctor, Tom Sewid, Echo Bay, Robson Bight, Boat Bay, Sointula, Mackenzie Sound, Port Hardy, Insect Island, Joe Cove, Mimkwamlis.

Alaska, however, still beckons and the way still is long. You can put it off, but if you are going, there is no way north except beyond the protection of Vancouver Island and across Queen Charlotte Strait, the first stretch of water open to the Pacific Ocean. The Inside Passage continues for another six hundred miles through some of the most remote and magnificent wilderness on the continent. It continues to be an adventure without parallel.

8 I Shot The Cougar

Shadow slips gently away from her dock, rounds the break-water, and heads north through San Juan Channel. Customs cleared at Bedwell Harbour, Nanaimo and Lund astern, through the Yuculta Rapids and soon the Inside Passage leads into wilderness. Beyond roads, television and newspapers, the comforts of civilization are left behind and we enter a world of challenge and opportunity. We find anchorages where ours is the only boat and wolves call from the protective mountains. We cross a line. Animals are no longer in our world; we are in their world. We exit center stage, the staged world defined by square lines, electronics, clocks and calendars. Now we see what's left of nature unravaged by civilization: salmon in their spawning streams, bears fishing for the salmon, orcas just cruising, and sea otters with their little rock and their young wrapped in seaweed. Free of the roles civilization has given us, we connect with the natural world and with a deep part of ourselves.

During the early years I learned to fish for salmon. Still in the basement are the rods, reels, nets, lines, hooks, and lures. There are few moments that get my attention quite as totally as the cry of "fish on" when the entire boat focuses on the catch. The other lines are brought in, the downriggers hauled out, the net readied. Brought on board, the gleaming, iridescent salmon seems to reflect all its life history from the smolt leaving its stream to feed and grow in the open ocean until it mysteriously and magically returns to its stream of origin four years later. Carefully killed and cleaned, the bright red flesh is as beautiful as the silver scales. Smoked over Alder wood, it blesses us.

In those early years I found great delight in the amazing profundity and variety of the sea: salmon, halibut, ling cod, rock cod, oysters, rock oysters, clams, prawns, abalone, scallops, crabs, sea cucumbers, urchins, moon snails, and herring roe. I ate them all. I also found great joy in feeding all of us on board with these wonders.

Getting dinner was pretty simple. We didn't even need bait to catch fish. Bill Brown and Clyde Hackler and I would fish boundary buoy out beyond Patos Island each fall using only lead weights with treble hooks. We poured the lead weights in a mold that Bill and Clyde had made in the University's technology workshop. Fishing three slack tides we would catch enough rock cod to fill our freezers for the winter. Dungeness crabs were also abundant. I found an old crab pot on the dock, fixed it up a bit, tied on a gallon plastic bottle for a float, baited it with a salmon head, loaded it in *Elsa*, and threw it into Bellingham Bay. I identified the spot by lining up two smoke stacks at the cement plant. When I wanted crab for dinner, I hauled up the pot, took out the crabs I wanted, threw the others back in, re-baited the pot and threw it back in too. There was no license required and no closed season. Back then it was considered standard operating procedure to get your dinner from another person's pot if your own was empty. Local protocol dictated the replacement of crabs with a six pack of beer or some other appropriate thank you.

In those days a season's fishing license in British Columbia was $20 for the boat. Whoever was on the boat could fish with that license. The limits were generous and we quit fishing when we got tired of catching. Clams were abundant and could be found on almost any beach. There were more oysters than you could imagine in Desolation Sound. I especially liked the oysters from the Ragged Islands or from a small pocket beach on Eveleigh Island. We had a smoker and canner on board, and the salmon that we could not keep fresh we smoked and canned for the winter. We also canned clams. A jar of smoked salmon or clams made a good Christmas present for my friends.

As the years passed the salmon and other sea life began to disappear. The destructive impact of commercial over-fishing, pollution, and habitat destruction became obvious and unavoidable. At the time, the change was almost imperceptible; actually it was quite precipitous. Salmon were the first to go. Herring balls, once commonplace, became rare. Abalone and scallops vanished. And then crabs and prawns were targeted by commercial fishermen, themselves struggling to survive. The proliferation of commercial crab pots clogged some of our favorite bays, making it impossible to anchor where before we had spent safe and peaceful nights. Even sea urchins and sea cucumbers were scooped up by divers who loaded them into totes trucked to the Asian markets in Vancouver. Gradually even the fishermen vanished. Where there were over a hundred commercial fishing boats in the harbor there are now three. Salmon no longer collect at Stuart Island. The resort is closed and Big Bay Marina has become a stopover for pleasure boaters.

As the ecological crisis deepened, environmental groups issued moralistic proclamations and governmental agencies generated futile and misguided regulations. Rather than address the causes of the collapse of an entire eco-system, the politicians and bureaucrats targeted the end users. Fishing was regulated, but the destruction of habitat by logging, commercial and municipal pollution, and commercial over-fishing, was left untouched under the guise of free enterprise and economic necessity.

As the tragedy became more and more obvious, I became more and more aware of my own contribution to the developing scarcity. I no longer fish at all--with or without bait. Making a virtue of a necessity, I joined the rising chorus of voices crying for relief for the beleaguered paradise we had known.

Fishing no longer fun, I looked for other excuses for being on the water. For a time I captained a whale-watching boat. Finding the orcas and watching as they played or fished or just coasted along was almost as exciting as pursuing salmon. They pretty much seemed to go about whatever business they were pursuing before we arrived. I always felt that the real threats to their well being were loss of the salmon they fed on, pollution, and underwater noise from commercial and military activity, and I felt that any contribution we made to their discomfort was offset by the education we were providing our passengers. We had a gifted naturalist aboard, and her narrations converted many tourists from observers to active environmental protectors. But as the whale watching "industry" grew, competition became more intense. We no longer went in search of the whales, we checked in with the industry network for a report on their location. You didn't look for the whales, you looked for the concentration of boats watching the whales. And, of course, with the proliferation of boats came regulations. At first they were voluntary, but then became law. So much distance from the whales, travel in the same direction they are going. Don't get between them and the shore, and on and on. And, with more competition, it became harder to make a living, so the owner of my boat cut expenses by dropping the educational component. At that point I felt that we were exploiting the whales and not returning fair value, so I quit working for her and started my own charter business, advertising it as "eco-adventure cruises."

Running a business was a new experience, but I thought we were off to a good start when a local environmental group, The Society for Interspecies Communication, chartered my boat. They wanted to take *Sundown* deep into British Columbia to spend a week studying the response of orca whales to various kinds of music. Using *Sundown* as a base for this project would be a learning experience for me, and it would be good for my new business. The association would certainly add credence to my charters as ecologically sensitive.

Departure day the group arrived on the dock beside *Sundown* with what looked like a boat-sinking load of musical instruments and electronic gear and a strong contingent of support crew. Jim Nollman, founder and director of the Society, and Katy Nollman and their daughters, Claire and Sasha, were there as well as Linda, Jill, Sandra, and Gene, all committed environmentalists. We loaded everyone and everything aboard *Sundown* and headed north.

I had asked my friend, Keith, to come along as first mate; Katy took charge of the galley. It was pretty much a cooperative venture and promised to be a delightful trip. While some of the crew took on galley chores, others worked with Jim on the musical and electronic gear, and everyone visited with Keith and me in the pilot house.

Our destination was Boat Bay on West Cracroft Island, near Port McNeill at the northern tip of Vancouver Island. The area is home to the northern resident orcas. Robson Bight, a famous hangout for the whales is nearby, and Paul and Helena Spong run OrcaLab from Hanson Island. Jim and Mary Bowerman operate the whale watching boats *Lukwa* and *Gikumi* out of Telegraph Cove and Bill and Donna Mackay operate *Naiad Explorer* out of Port McNeill. The location was perfect; the annual return of the resident pods was predictable and rewarding.

The Society for Interspecies Communication had been to Boat Bay on several previous occasions so Jim directed me to an anchorage just off the beach at the southern end of the bay. A pocket beach was tucked behind a rocky point that protected it from the wind and currents in Johnston Strait. At high tide, there was almost no beach at all, but at low tide there were sand, rocks, and tide pools to explore. A small level area above high tide was just large enough for a campfire, picnic table and kitchen area. Beyond that, as with most Northwest beaches, the forest of alder, fir, hemlock and madrona closed in, allowing only scattered clearings big enough for a tent. The deep water of Johnston Strait swirled outside the point and the orcas frequently swam past within a few feet of the cliff.

Sundown's anchor set, we launched the skiff and began to ferry ashore all the paraphernalia of the camp: tents, kitchen supplies, food, sleeping bags, clothing, and musical instruments. Driftwood tables and benches, fanciful totems and shamanistic emblems, and other useful and not so useful mementos from the group's previous visits were drug out of the woods and within hours a comfortable beach-side camp was established. On one of those earlier visits the group had named the place "Orcananda." If ever a place lent itself to an integration of humans with their natural world, this was it.

Jim and the other musicians set up their sound system aboard *Sundown* and brought their guitars and flutes ashore. The fire crackled. Keith, Katy, Linda and Gene produced coffee and food. *Sundown* rested comfortably at anchor.

Around the campfire talk turned to earlier visits to Boat Bay and to various efforts to establish communication with the whales. Previous groups had included Tibetan monks who chanted with the whales, violins, marimba drums, and all sorts of other musical offerings.

By the fourth day at Orcananda, we had settled into an idyllic routine. Mostly vegetarian meals were enhanced with an occasional fresh entrée from the abundance of Johnston Strait, a salmon, ling cod, or clams. Mornings and early afternoons were devoted to gentle camp chores and leisure time for talk, coffee, writing or exploring the shoreline or woods. We watched Linda attract ravens to the rocky shore with bits of food and amazingly accurate whistles and calls. Late afternoons and evenings were devoted to the whales that appeared with reassuring regularity. At bedtime Keith and I returned to *Sundown* and the others to their tents scattered just beyond the perimeter of the camp area.

On the fourth morning, we were having after-breakfast coffee around the campfire and discussing whatever important or trivial topics people discuss when they are free to let their minds and words wander where they will. Then wham! Our quiet lassitude was shattered by intense, demanding screams: "Help, help, help me, help me." Our reverie collapsed, we were snapped into the present, frozen as we tried to define the danger, then mobilized into response as we realized that the cries for help came from the woods just beyond the edge of the camp area.

Without a word between us, we headed in the direction of the screams. The trail at the edge of the camp quickly turned into a single file path between almost impenetrable walls of salal. I was in the lead. As I rounded a bend in the trail the source of danger burst upon us. A cougar crouched directly ahead, blocking the trail. He was staring at us.

I froze. This was experience beyond my edge, outside my range. A cougar is not a large bob-cat. This was a real lion--a mountain lion. His sleek, tan, muscular body completely filled the narrow path. His head was larger than mine. His cat eyes were clear and unblinking. I was mesmerized and immobilized.

Linda, the raven lady, was behind me. She pushed my confusion and hesitation aside, picked up a small stick from somewhere, and attacked the cougar with it. After repeated blows, she drove him into the salal. I was as stunned by her performance as was the cougar. Linda led us down the trail to a small beach where a trickle of fresh water made its way to the tide line. Jill lay in the stream, bleeding, but calm and coherent. She had been kneeling to wash her hair in the stream when the cougar attacked. At first she played dead as the books had instructed. But he had continued to maul her, biting her head and leg and he would have killed her if her screams had not distracted him and brought us.

Although Jill's wounds were serious and needed medical attention, her life was not in danger. They were mostly puncture wounds, not bleeding alarmingly, and she was not going into shock. As two of us helped her along the tide line back to camp, the rest of us returned by the trail. We were wet, adrenaline pumped, and confused. Jim said he had just seen the cougar again; the great cat was still in the camp area.

My attention was divided between the need to get medical help for Jill and the threat of the cougar. I asked Keith to go to *Sundown* and bring the guns ashore. I asked the others if they would agree to stay in the campfire area and leave only with Keith or me as protection until we had taken care of Jill and determined our situation more calmly. Everyone agreed.

After determining that others were taking good care of Jill, I began to radio for help. It was a little over twenty miles to Port McNeill, the closest medical facility. To get *Sundown* underway and to Port McNeill would take at least three hours. I knew there were fast whale watch boats in the area that could make the trip in less than an hour. It was not long before help began to arrive. A medical doctor from one of the boats in the area arrived and confirmed our judgment that Jill's wounds were sufficiently bandaged for the time being but that she needed to go to a hospital. Bill McKay, aboard his whale watch boat *Naiad Explorer*, sent a skiff and offered a fast trip for Jill to Port McNeill and the hospital there. Linda volunteered to accompany Jill and they were on their way. After excellent medical attention in Port McNeill, Jill decided to return home immediately by land.

Meanwhile, back at Orcananda our radio message had been picked up by others in the area and shortly there was a hum of activity. A group of whale researchers camped at the north end of Boat Bay arrived in their outboard. Paul and Helena Spong from OrcaLab on Hanson Island sent a boat. For a time it seemed as if the entire south end of Boat Bay was grid locked with outboard motors and people talking on radios.

Gradually the boat and radio traffic diminished and those of us who were left began to examine our own situation. With Jill safe, our concern was the cougar. Why had this usually secretive cat attacked in broad daylight? Was he still in the camp area? We all had our ideas and theories. Did the cougar think that Jill, kneeling down, was one of the children? That made us shudder. What were we going to do next? Should we all move to the boat? Should we call the game warden? Should we call the coast guard? Should we abandon the whole project? Our adrenaline high led us on and on.

Eventually, one of the Nollman children wanted a sweater from her tent. Still operating with our interim regulations, I retrieved the Winchester 30/30 from its resting place near the kitchen area and accompanied Katy and her daughter. About fifty feet from camp, the cougar crouched, staring at us. After all the noise and confusion, this wild animal was still stalking us. I sent Katy and her daughter back to camp and asked them to send Keith. Keith arrived with the 12 gauge and accompanied by Sandra, one of the Society for Inter-Species Communication members. The three of us knelt behind a large log and watched the cougar. He was sitting, looking right at us, not moving.

Thoughts were running through my mind at a thousand bits per second. Why was this animal still around the camp? Why was he unafraid? Why was he not running from us now? Should I shoot him? I knew that the game warden or wildlife ranger would be here later today or tomorrow. And I knew that they would try to kill the cougar. It had already attacked a human and was therefore a dangerous animal. There was no use in trapping him and removing him to the wilderness; this was the wilderness. What would we do in the meantime? What were the Canadian laws governing this situation? Would I be breaking the law if I killed the cougar? What would I tell people if I didn't kill him and he later attacked someone else?

I checked out my own condition. I knew my weapon. It was the 30/30 Winchester that I had hunted with since I was twelve years old. I was relaxed, not breathing fast. I had an excellent shot--about forty feet. The cougar was not moving, but looking right at me. I knew the game warden would never get a better shot. I knew Jim Nollman would not be happy. The last thing he said was, "Please don't shoot him." I asked Keith what he thought. He was as ambivalent as I was. Quietly Sandra said, "I have communicated with the cougar. He says it is OK to kill him." I didn't know quite what to do with this bit of information.

What finally tipped the balance for me was the thought of how I would feel if I did not kill him and he attacked another person. I also knew that there was something extraordinarily odd about this great cat's continued presence so close to camp. I wondered if he was rabid.

Time took on a strange dimension. While all these thoughts were flying around, there was also a context of calm and ease. It was a combination of steady concentration and at the same time processing lots of data and options. We were on the brink of a precipice, but had time to consider whether or not to jump. Again I checked myself. I was in good shooting condition. I steadied my arm against the log and put the cross hairs in my scope right on the cougar's mouth. I squeezed off a shot. The results were spectacular. The huge cat exploded ten feet straight up. I remember thinking about how long his tail was. He dropped to the ground, stone still. I knew I had killed him with one shot to the head.

The three of us walked toward the crumpled body.

When we were three feet from him the cougar exploded again.

He was not dead, only stunned. Now time assumed a different guise. I was confused and frustrated. The present was collapsed. The cat disappeared into the thick brush in an instant. He went straight up the cliff, through the most difficult terrain. I had made a serious and dangerous mistake. Assuming that the first shot had killed the cat, I was unprepared for a second shot. Keith and I chased the big cat, but we were no match. We saw some drops of blood. We ran until we were exhausted. Repeatedly we caught our breath and ran again. We never saw him.

The next morning the game warden arrived early, along with the RCMP, Fish and Wildlife authorities, a professional tracker, dogs, and lots of guns. They searched all day for the cougar without success. The following day they returned with more people, another tracker, more dogs, and more guns. Again they searched all day and again they found no trace of the big cat.

At the place where I had hit the cougar the tracker found some teeth fragments, hair, and porcupine quills. That explained a lot. Evidently my bullet had fragmented when it hit the cougar's teeth, thus causing pain but not a critical injury. And evidently the cougar had a mouth full of porcupine quills, explaining his peculiar behavior.

While the authorities searched for the cougar, the inhabitants of Orcanada attempted to bring some order into the chaos of the past three days. They had been busy days: Jill's screams; the race to the beach; the cougar in our midst; Jill's injuries and evacuation; the guns; emergency procedures; the radios, boats, outboards; the wounding of the still present cougar; the authorities with guns and dogs. On top of all this add the talk, speculation, analysis, the uncertainty about the condition of the cougar and about our own safety, the futile searches, more talk, more speculation, more analysis.

Our emotional condition was palpable and the accumulated intensity which had so far been contained by the need for action began to boil to the surface. Individually and as a group we attempted over and over to process the events and our feelings. We were not an ordinary group. All of us were devoted to the protection of wild animals and their territory. We had deep feelings about the sanctity of all life and felt a special responsibility for protecting wildlife that was increasingly pressed by encroaching human expansion. At the same time there was an awareness of danger the cougar presented.

Time shifted again and a strange process of justification began. Reflection replaced action and with reflection came second thoughts, questions, opinions and rationalizations. Uncertainty and ambiguity gave way to judgment and defensiveness. Imperceptibly the focus of the group shifted from the cougar attack on Jill to my decision to shoot him, and I became a part of the problem rather than a part of the solution. Had I acted correctly given the responsibility that was mine, or had I usurped authority and acted against the purposes and intentions of the group. Shared participation in a complex set of conditions and actions mutated into an adversarial tension. Genuine communication evaporated and was replaced by rationalization and moralizing. We all tried to break through this shell of fear, but we could not.

The day after the authorities left, a dispirited group of interspecies communicators packed up and left Orcananda. We cruised up to Bond Sound and attempted to salvage something from the trip, but gloom hung over us like a blanket. We all tried to discuss the issue, but the communication did not happen. We were disappointed, depressed, and demoralized. There was a feeling that our ethical universe had been violated. I was defensive. I felt I was being judged unfairly. I felt the others blanked out my feelings of ambiguity as well as their own, and in the luxury of reflective space polarized the situation. I also felt they failed to put themselves in my position as captain of the boat, with special responsibility for the safety of the group. Between the Scylla of judgment and the Charybdis of defensiveness, the promise of Orcanada floundered and our group cohesion and mutuality collapsed. Even as I retell this story after a decade, I feel my defensiveness rise again. How can I tell this story without my own needs for self justification intruding?

On the way back to Friday Harbor there were several more efforts to debrief the situation and the events. But they never went anywhere. I continued to feel that I had acted ethically and responsibly but the consensus of the group was clearly otherwise. The high spirits with which we began had been destroyed not by the cougar, not by Jill's injury, nor by my shooting the cougar, but by our inability to live creatively and constructively with our differences.

It has been twelve years since the cougar attack at Boat Bay. Still, today, in the top right hand drawer of my desk is a film case containing bits of hair, tooth fragments and pieces of lead bullet. Although I have thought about it and told the story many times, this is the first time I've written about it. From this distant perspective I now think that our disillusionment and inability to get on top of this event was rooted deeper than the cougar attack. Consciously or unconsciously we realized that the cougar event was a microcosm of the larger issues of eco-system survival. Our best efforts to preserve a delicate balance within an ecosystem--whales, salmon, cougars, crabs, sea cucumbers--are thwarted by our own presence.

The cougar at Orcanada became a part of the lore of the region. I never anchored again in Boat Bay, but on return visits to the area, sometimes I was asked about those events. Two years later I received a phone call from a person who lived in the area and knew the lore. He wanted me to know that a man living on West Cracroft Island had recently shot a cougar who was stalking his young daughters in their back yard and that the cougar was a female and had a deformed jaw.

"No culture has yet solved the dilemma each has faced with the growth of a conscious mind: how to live a moral and compassionate existence when one is fully aware of the blood, the horror inherent in all life, when one finds darkness not only in one's own culture but within oneself. If there is a stage at which an individual life becomes truly adult, it must be when one grasps the irony in its unfolding and accepts responsibility for a life lived in the midst of such paradox. One must live in the middle of contradiction because if all contradiction were eliminated at once life would collapse. There are simply no answers to some of the great pressing questions. You continue to live them out, making your life a worthy expression of a leaning into the light."

--Barry Lopez, <u>Arctic Dreams</u>

9 CHRYSLER PETE'S

When I bought *Elsa* the Bellingham airport was a one-room cinder-block building and Chrysler Pete's was the only chandlery in town. Redden Net and Lummi Fishery Supply were not there yet, and West Marine was years in the future. Doc Freeman's was still in business on Lake Union in Seattle and you could order things by phone from them and the people you talked to were knowledgeable and helpful, but if you actually wanted to handle stuff it was Chrysler Pete's. "Chrysler" because for years Pete was a dealer for Chrysler Crown Marine engines but that was before my time, and "Pete's" because the owner's last name was Peterson. I didn't know what his first name was until much later when I found out it was Jules. But anyway, everybody called him Pete and so it really didn't matter. I also learned much later that Pete was born on Christmas Eve in 1903 in Tacoma and that his parents had come from Norway around 1898. But I didn't know any of that at the time.

To get to Chrysler Pete's you took "C" street across Holly and the railroad tracks and just past Industrial Electric turned left into the gravel parking lot. Pete's was the small clapboard building with pealing grey/green paint. Inside there was a wood stove in the corner to the right of the door as you came in and a couch and a couple of chairs and you could bring a cup of coffee from somewhere else and sit there and talk with whoever else came in and even sometimes with Pete. But those were rare occasions when Pete would take a few minutes off to chat. Usually he was busy moving stuff around on the shelves or answering questions for customers or at the cash register.

Wellcraft Shipyard was still in business then and they had a marine railway, but for hauling smaller boats, it was Pete's--one boat at a time. There were no travel lifts in Bellingham then but Pete had designed and built his own marine elevator. It was a platform that Pete lowered into the water and you just drove your boat over it. Everything was run by a four cylinder Ford engine, salvaged from an ancient car or truck and only Pete could start and operate it. Then, through an amazing collection of gears, drums, cables, and pulleys, the platform would rise out of the water with your boat aboard. Terry, Pete's son, would climb down over the creosote pole bulkhead and adjust the blocks under the keel and other supports and then the platform would continue up until it was almost level with the land. And there your boat was, high and dry, but still over the water.

This was, of course, before the EPA existed and no one thought much about scraping off the old bottom paint and putting on new over the water. When the lift was lowered and the boat went back in the water, the tide carried all the remains away. Anyway, they were soon lost in the effluent that was discharged by the huge Georgia-Pacific paper mill next door.

After the boat was out of the water you could go inside Pete's store and buy Old Sailor copper paint and scrapers, rollers, brushes, thinner and whatever else you needed. There were also zincs, oakum, flax for stuffing boxes, bronze pipe fittings, galvanized screws, and even a few cutlass bearings. Pete had a small prop shop and he would loan you a prop puller and then take out the dings and dents. He could also straighten a bent shaft. Dust masks, ear protectors, disposable gloves?---You gotta be kidding. You just jumped down to the elevator over the water and went to work.

I always liked to haul out Memorial Day weekend because Pete didn't charge lay days over weekends and holidays. That meant I got three free days and with my three sons helping we could usually get the work done. It was only years later that I learned how much those guys hated Memorial Day, which was a holiday they didn't get to celebrate at the park with their friends but when they helped Dad paint the boat. I thought they were having fun with me.

The first couple of years I hauled at Pete's and bought stuff there and asked questions and sought Pete's advice, I always felt like he resented my being there. Although he would give me good advice, he seemed distant and acted as if it were the first time he had ever seen me. But after about three years, Pete's attitude changed. He recognized me and even remembered my name. I've thought about that, and I've decided that at first Pete just didn't want to waste time on someone who didn't seem to know much about boats and who probably wouldn't be around long anyway. But once he realized that I was going to be permanent and that I was going to learn what I needed to know, he decided I was worth the effort. The first time Pete called me by name I felt like the time I graduated from college and the dean called my name to come to the stage and receive my diploma. I really knew I had arrived when it got to be OK for me to go back into the shop area and look for a tool or something I needed or just to watch what was going on there.

Terry worked in the prop shop out back and I didn't see much of him until Pete started to think about retiring and Terry started to work up front more. Eventually when Pete retired Terry ran the place. Well, Pete never really retired until he died and Terry never really ran it because it was always Chrysler Pete's. But when I was hauling out there for annual maintenance, Terry ran the prop shop and blocked up the boats when they were hauled.

I really don't know for sure about any of this concerning Terry and Pete because you never know what really goes on between a father and a son, but this is the way it looked to me from the outside.

Terry created a small maritime museum in a room to the left of the main room as you came in the front door of the shop. Gradually Pete began to retreat into the background and Terry took over more and more of the business just about the time the EPA decided scraping off old bottom paint directly over the water was not such a good idea. Georgia Pacific was also having trouble with what it was dumping into Bellingham Bay by the thousands of gallons and they built a long, large pipeline to dump stuff further out in the bay and then they built a large settling basin to settle out the really bad stuff. I was never very clear about what happened to the bad stuff then, but that's another story.

One day, when Pete was pretty old and Terry was running the shop, Pete climbed up on the roof to fix a leak and then he fell off. Pete was really tall and skinny and Terry said he looked like a stepped on daddy long-legs spider lying in the driveway. Terry called the ambulance and they loaded Pete up and headed for the hospital, but before they got out of the driveway, they stopped and backed up. The attendant came in and told Terry that when Pete found out how much the ambulance cost, he refused to go. So although Terry was pretty pissed off and had to lock up the store, they loaded Pete into his truck and Terry took him to the hospital.

Between Lummi Fishery Supply, Redden Net, West Marine and the EPA, Chrysler Pete's didn't stand much of a chance. Terry tried to keep things going because he really loved the place, as did many of us, and he loved the museum and the prop shop, but he was just trying to push water uphill. Finally Chrysler Pete's closed and the museum stuff was donated to the Whatcom Maritime Society, but it wasn't the same and I think Terry missed the old days even if Pete was always in the background and so he finally went to work for Hardware Sales.

Thinking about those times and trying to write about them, I called Terry to get some information. We talked for a long time and I could tell that he held some of these memories as close as I do. I could hear it in his voice as he told me some more things about his dad and the museum. About the first thing he said was "You will include something about Joe won't you?" I already knew that Joe would be in the story, but for Terry, Joe was at the top of the list.

Joe was Bellingham's first street person before being a street person was a way of life. Joe lived around the docks during the summer, sleeping in some convenient corner or cardboard box, and in the winter moved into the Lighthouse Mission just up "C" street. Summer and winter, Joe wore a hunter's cap with a bill and ear flaps and lined with fake sheepskin. He was always bundled in a bunch of scruffy shirts, pants, and coats and always wore gum boots. His hat, clothing, and what you could see of his hands and face wore indelible dirt. People who didn't know Joe would find him a bit frightening or scary or even dangerous, but actually Joe was a harmless as a kitten and just as shy. He wouldn't talk to anyone but Terry, and if you spoke to him it would scare him and he would run away. He was a shadow or a ghost. The ghost of the dock. But, as I've heard is true with many real ghosts, after a while you got used to his being around, and let ghostly things just be what they were.

Each morning when I returned to work on my boat, all of the bits and pieces of the previous day's work would be carefully lined up on a beam or at the edge of the work area. Bottle caps, bits of wood, bent bolts, rusted washers and forgotten tools--Joe had picked them all up and lined them up. Sometimes I would see him lurking at the corner of the building.

The closest I ever got to Joe was to buy a can of coke from the machine outside the back door of the prop shop and put it on a piling over at the side of the yard. Joe would watch and eventually go get it. He would drink half and pour the rest over the side of the pier into the water. Terry said he always poured half his drink or scraped half his food into the ocean to return it to the fish. Joe got a small check from somewhere each month and Terry would cash it for him and give him a few dollars each week. He never knew what Joe did with the money until he began to find cans of green beans hidden everywhere around the yard--in the water meter box, under the dumpster, in between pilings, can after can of green beans. Terry talked to the owner of the mom and pop grocery up on Holly street and the owner there said that at the first of each week Joe would buy cans of beans. He always wondered what he did with them.

Terry told me that earlier in his life Joe had been an accountant. But then something happened. No one knew for sure. But Joe, in his childlike and harmless shyness, seemed to be happy. He was very much a part of Chrysler Pete's and of the docks there at Squalicum Harbor in those days. Maybe we were all more childlike and happier, too.

10 CROSSING THE STRAIT: ALERT BAY TO BELLA BELLA

Alert Bay to Wells Passage--24 miles
Wells Passage to Cape Caution--51 miles
Cape Caution to Penrose Island--20 miles
Penrose Island to Pruth Anchorage--21 miles
Pruth Ancorage to the Koeye River--12 miles
The Koeye River to Lizzie Cove--23 miles
Lizzie Cove to Bella Bella--8 miles

Queen Charlotte Strait, like Georgia Strait and the Yuculta Rapids, is a transition point on the Inside Passage. After leaving the protection of Vancouver Island, the comforting and familiar symbols of society and security rapidly fall away. Marinas, repair facilities, yacht clubs, radio chatter, and crowded anchorages become rare. The signs of our own culture are replaced by the rich cultures of First Nations. Wildlife comes to the fore. Orcas, salmon, grizzlies, wolves, coyotes and eagles are in charge here.

Queen Charlotte Strait is also the point of no return. Once across the Strait, it is about as easy to keep going as it is to turn

Bella Bella

Lizzy Cove

Koeye River

Pruth
Anchorage

Penrose
Island

Cape Caution   Wells Passage

Queen Charlotte Strait

Alert Bay

Queen Charlotte
Sound

God's Pocket

Vancouver
Island

N

Scale in Miles

0   10   20   30   40   50   100

back. Within the next three hundred miles Shearwater, near Bella Bella, is the only repair facility. Not until Prince Rupert and Highway 16 is there ground transportation back home. There is an airport in Bella Bella with connections to Vancouver. That's about it.

British Columbia Ferries provide twice weekly ferry service between Port Hardy and Prince Rupert with a stop in Bella Bella. Until March, 2006, this remote ferry route was served by the *Queen of the North*, flagship of the British Columbia fleet. She was beautiful, graceful, 410 feet long, and carried 700 passengers. *Queen of the North* was an icon, symbolizing connections between the isolated villages and settlements of the north coast and the rest of the world. To meet her in Grenville Channel or to hear Prince Rupert Traffic advise us that she would overtake *Sundown* in Fitzhugh Sound was comforting, like meeting an old friend.

Shortly after midnight on March 22, 2006, in gale winds and six foot seas *Queen of the North* hit Gil Rock off Juan Point in Wright Sound. She sank within an hour in 1000 feet of water; a reminder, among other things, of how quickly the shores in these waters drop off into the dark deep. In spite of the late hour and storm conditions, fishermen in the First Nations village of Hartley Bay, seven miles to the north, responded immediately to the mayday call from *Queen of the North*. While they pushed their gillnetters and purse seiners through heavy seas toward the stricken *Queen*, those who stayed at home began to prepare food and collect blankets for survivors. The Canadian Coast Guard vessel, *Sir Wilfred Laurier*, anchored in Barnard Harbour, fifteen miles to the south, also responded, as did a number of Canadian Coast Guard helicopters and other vessels. Of 101 passengers and crew aboard, ninety-nine were rescued. Two were unaccounted for and presumed drowned.

Queen of the North hit Gil Island at full speed of 17.5 knots. When *Queen of the North* entered Wright Sound from Grenville Channel, she should have made a small course correction to port. She did not do so. Investigations by various Canadian agencies concluded that human error was to blame. The bridge crew was not sufficiently aware of the exact location of the vessel and did not properly make the course correction nor verify that it had been made. The navigating officer, quarter master, and helmswoman were on the bridge at the time. The two officers, who had recently concluded a romantic relationship, were engaged in a "personal discussion." When Gill Island loomed out of the darkness, it was too late.

There are lessons here for all of us.

· When something goes wrong operator error is usually to blame.

· A combination of small mistakes can result in large catastrophes.

· The fool catcher is never far away.

· As my mentor, Walt Masland, said when I bragged about the size of my new command, *Sundown*, at sixty-four feet and eighty-one tons, "Don't forget Joseph, in the ocean they are all small boats."

Hopefully remembering these lessons, the traditional route for small boats leaving the protection of Vancouver Island lies across the open waters of Queen Charlotte Sound. The route passes Pine Island, Cape Caution and Egg Island with its famous light house. Unlike the United States, Canada continues to staff its lighthouses and the light keepers on Egg Island sometimes exchange sea condition information with passing boats on VHF channel 09. This frequently unpleasant and sometimes dangerous 45 mile crossing finally ends inside Cape Calvert at Safety

Cove or Pruth Anchorage. The transit calls for a very early departure, before daylight if possible. On my last crossing I left at 0430. It's open water with no place to hide.

In the past, I have left from God's Pocket, Port McNeill, Port Hardy, and Alert Bay. But my favorite departure point is Port Alexander, a large, safe, uninhabited anchorage on Nigei Island. Starting here shortens the crossing by about twenty miles. From Port Alexander I turn north through Browning Passage between Balaklava Island and Nigei Island and in less than an hour, from Cardigan Rocks in Gordon Channel I get a good idea of what the weather in the Strait is like. If the seas don't look friendly, I just go back to Port Alexander, catch a couple of rock cod, set out the crab traps, and have a good lay day.

The goal is Cape Calvert. On those rare crossings when the sea is calm and the sky blue, it's a great trip. There's nothing out there but water, so, with iron mike at the helm and no rocks or landmasses anywhere close, there is plenty of time for relaxing in the sun on the foredeck, boat chores, and a short nap for those not on watch. Unfortunately sunny weather and calm seas are the exception rather than the rule. More frequently those long swells from the Pacific with a chop on top, while not dangerous for the boat, induce fantasies of suicide in her crew. The crossing seems endless; everyone yearns for anchorage.

Safety Cove, five miles inside Cape Calvert provides the first protection. But the place is misnamed because, actually, it is quite deep, the holding bottom is uncertain and protection limited. Penrose Island, with several good anchorages is a better idea. It's only twenty-one miles from Penrose to Pruth Bay. Until about ten years ago, Pruth was a favorite stop. The anchorage was seldom crowded and frequently deserted. It was just a short walk along a good path, past a famous mask carved on a tree, to marvelous beaches on the exposed westerly side of Calvert Island. If the sun was out, it was easy to imagine yourself on a South Pacific island: white sandy beaches, small islets in the distance. Our hunts for treasure on the beach were sometimes rewarded with olive shells, reinforcing the illusion of the South Pacific. Two of these small, beautiful shells hang on the wall near my bed.

But time and progress have seriously undermined Kwakshua's appeal. About ten years ago someone built a large, upscale fishing lodge on Pruth Bay. The idea was to provide upscale accommodation for fishermen who flew in to fish for the famous Kings in Hakai Passage. With outside civilization encroaching, everything changed. The trail and the mask are still there, and although the lodge owners permit visitors to cross their land, the feeling of freedom, wilderness and mystery has vanished.

Ironically, the lodge was barely finished before the fishing collapsed. Now it belongs to new owners who are planning a visitor-friendly retreat center.

More fishing lodges and significantly fewer salmon are not the only changes during the past decade. GPS and pin-point accurate electronic charts changed the way I cross the Strait. For years, tug boats and people with local knowledge had avoided the long crossing by taking another route close to the mainland. The distance and exposure were about the same, but in bad weather they could seek shelter in one of several inlets or bays such as Blunden Harbour, Marsh Bay, Jeannette Islands, Shelter Bay, Allison Harbour, Miles Inlet, or Smith Sound. This route, however, had never appealed to me. The entrances to most of these protected anchorages are littered with rocks, and without local knowledge, especially in poor weather, it would have been difficult and dangerous. Better the open water.

With a GPS and electronic charts, these sites of refuge suddenly became accessible. Now I leave the protection of the Broughton Archipelago through Wells Passage. The anchorages along the way provide comfort if the weather gods are angry. Once past Dugout Rocks, I head for the delightful anchorage inside Fury Island or to Frypan Bay or Big Frypan Bay on Penrose Island.

North of Queen Charlotte Strait, the Inside Passage winds 250 miles through the Great Bear Rainforest. Lying between Knight Inlet and the Alaskan border, this is the largest intact temperate rainforest in the world. It is the home of the largest grizzlies in Canada, of coastal wolves, and of almost countless runs of salmon. It is also the home of the Spirit Bear.

On my earliest trips to Alaska, I hurried through this stretch, unaware of its magnificence. Here, on the North Coast of British Columbia, the coastal range meets the ocean. The inlets are deep and the anchorages few. While the waters are relatively protected, rain is a constant companion and gray skies are the norm. It is, after all, a rainforest. Like many other travelers, passing as quickly as possible over the deep and empty anchorages and intimidating settlements, I rushed to the relative security and familiarity of Ketchikan.

Then I met Karen and Ian McAllister, environmental activists, organizers, photographers, writers, research biologists, visionaries, and, more recently, parents. Although younger than my own children, Karen and Ian became not only my friends but also my teachers. They took me to the Koeye River, Troop Narrows and Kynoch Inlet. Day after day, year after year, they opened my eyes to both the beauty and the fragility of their world. Over the next few years, they showed me what I had been missing and introduced me to this most fascinating and neglected portion of the Inside Passage. Ian showed me how to anchor on the sand bar at the head of Khutze Inlet, where the current from the river would hold *Sundown* steady on her anchor. And he showed me where it was safe to anchor at the head of Aaltanhash Inlet, beneath the high waterfall, a deep anchorage, but secure. Karen taught me where to find bear grass and how to prepare its rice-sized tubers and collect wild greens for a fresh salad--no preservatives or additives, no pesticides or fertilizers. We soaked at the tide line in the 100 degree water of remote Tallheo Hot Springs on the way to Bella Coola, and swam in the shallow and sun-warmed water at Gunboat Pass. We visited Kwakumi Inlet, Namu, Kisameet Bay, Lucy Bay, Evans Inlet, Yeo Island, Pooley Island, Klekane Inlet, Green Inlet, and Gribbell Island. As we hiked up the Aaltanhash River, Karen and Ian showed me hemlock rubbing trees where grizzly and black bears had left hair in the bark. We visited Princess Royal Island, the home of the Spirit Bear.

Not only did Karen and Ian introduce me to the magnificence of the Great Bear Rainforest, they also opened a window for me into the fragile vulnerability of this magnificent forest world. For decades the North Coast has been exploited and damaged by logging, mining, hunting and most recently by fish farms and the threat of oil tankers.

Karen and Ian first visited the North Coast in 1990. In 1991 they founded the Raincoast Conservation Society, and later Pacific Wild. For the past sixteen years the Great Bear Rainforest has been their home and its preservation their work. Since arriving aboard their catamaran, *Companion*, they have built a home near Bella Bella and devoted themselves to protecting the environment and life style of this magic place. Karen and Ian are not arm-chair environmentalists. They have hiked up each of the 114 watersheds between Knight Inlet and Prince Rupert. Their book, The Great Bear Rainforest, full of awe-inspiring photographs and thoughtful, passionate text, has been a staple in my boat's library ever since it was publish in 1997. Ian's new book, The Last Wild Wolves, is equally mesmerizing. They have raised hundreds of thousands of dollars in their efforts to protect the North Coast from logging and they have initiated unprecedented and critically important basic research about coastal grizzlies, wolves, and salmon.

At first it was the logging. Vast tracts have been carelessly clear cut: Pooley Island, James Bay, Walbran Island, Yeo Island, Draney Inlet, Roderick Island, Tom Bay, Gibble Island, Ingram Lake. No thought was given to the environment. The forests were logged down to the tideline and across streams, destroying salmon spawning beds, creating erosion, and destroying habitat for bears, wolves, and salmon.

The remoteness of the Great Bear Rainforest is a two edged sword. Its isolation made logging expensive and the logging companies left it alone until areas closer to mills, like Vancouver Island, had been exhausted. At the same time, once logging was in full swing, marshaling opposition was more difficult. The isolation of the rainforest became a liability. Because the sites were so remote, the loggers could clear cut and leave slash as they wished. It is hard to organize a protest or gain publicity when the only ways into the logging sites are float plane or private boat.

For several years, *Sundown* became a bit player. We brought individuals and representatives from the Sierra Club, NRDC, and other organizations into the Great Bear Rainforest. With Karen and Ian as guides, we were able to show a few people the damage that had been done by the logging companies-- Interfor, Western Forest Products, Macmillan Blodel, and West Frasier. In some ways it was Catch 22. As the opposition to the clear cutting became more pronounced, the loggers speeded up their destruction knowing that their time was limited.

During the past two years, after seemingly endless meetings, protests, demonstrations, letters, and campaigns, the B.C. Government has announced several steps designed to protect portions of the wilderness. Exactly how ecologically significant these protected areas are and how these actions actually play out remains to be seen.

The Great Bear Rainforest is home to the largest grizzly bears in Canada. And, therefore, it is a world class trophy hunting destination. Sportsmen from all over the world pay tens of thousands of dollars for the experience of killing one of these great animals. "Hunting" usually means sitting in a blind constructed by a guide and waiting for a bear, previously observed and studied by the guide, to come along a defined path. In December, 2005, in cooperation with five First Nations, the Raincoast Conservation Society bought the trophy hunting licenses for a region of 20,000 square kilometers, limiting trophy hunting. The price was $1,350,000. Management of hunting licenses was turned over to the local First Nations people. The victory was incomplete however and the struggle to end trophy killing in the Great Bear Rainforest continues.

If it's not one thing it's another. Now fish farming threatens the balance and stability of the eco-system of the rainforest. We have known for a long time that salmon are dependent on the forest to provide shade, stability and protection to their fragile spawning beds. Water depth, speed, temperature, and clarity;

texture of the gravel bottom; and forest protection are all critical and must remain constant within very small tolerances. We have watched television programs about salmon hatcheries with roe in trays and sperm squirted over it, assuming that this artificial insemination could take the place of natural processes. Now we know that hatchery breeding seriously reduces genetic diversity, leaving the salmon vulnerable to disease and environmental forces. We have also begun to realize how rare and precious the natural process is, and how critical the various parameters are. Stream temperature must not vary more than a degree or two, the gravel must be just right. The environment that supports life is very fragile. Moreover, we have begun to learn that the forest is also dependent on the salmon. Salmon carcasses, carried into the forest by bears and wolves, are a significant source of fertilizer essential for the health of the huge trees. The dependence of the entire eco-system on the nutrients provided by spawned out salmon is only now beginning to be understood.

There are over 130 fish farms on the British Columbia Coast, with hundreds more planned. Most are owned by Scandinavian companies. These farms, using net pens between 30 and 100 feet in diameter and 30 to 60 feet deep, produce hundreds of thousands of non-native, Atlantic salmon. They also produce hundreds of thousands of pounds of toxic waste products. High concentrations of nitrogen from uneaten food and offal create hot spots under each farm. One by-product is a serious infestation of sea lice which attack native fish passing through these narrow channels between the open ocean and their spawning streams. This infestation of sea lice contributed to a 98% collapse of wild Pink salmon runs in this region in 2002. In addition, salmon that escape the fish farm net pens threaten to displace native populations. The high nitrogen hot spots also contribute to toxic algae blooms. And, of course, farmed fish do not provide food for bears and wolves and do not fertilize the forests. As human food, farmed salmon contain artificial color, harmful hormones, and toxic chemicals. Besides that, they taste bad. Farmed fish lack the subtlety and complexity of the forest, the rivers, and the ocean that make wild salmon one of the rare and truly awe inspiring gifts of the sea.

Recently European salmon viruses have been detected in both wild and farmed British Columbia Salmon. These viruses destroyed salmon populations in South America years ago and now threaten Canadian and American salmon. Alexandra Morton, from Alert Bay, has documented the evidence. The B.C. government and the fish farms have tried to conceal it.

Basic scientific research supports Karen and Ian's activism. Pacific Wild is exploring ecologically sustainable and gastronomically acceptable alternatives to open pen farms. In another project, teams of Pacific Wild volunteers are collecting wolf scat from the most remote islands, closest to the open Pacific. These thousands of specimens are shipped to research labs for analysis. The result seems to establish the B. C. coastal wolves as a distinct sub-species.

The most recent threat to the Great Bear Rain Forest comes from a proposal by Enbridge Oil Company to build a pipeline from the Alberta Tar Fields to Kitimat at the head of Douglas Channel. They intend loading more than 220 giant oil freighters per year to transport dangerous heavy crude oil through narrow passages to markets in Asia. The proposed route for these huge oil freighters, some four times the size of *Queen of the North*, is through Wright Sound and past Gil Island, exactly where the

Queen ran aground and sank. As I write, this controversy is very much alive. Enbridge is moving ahead with its project. First Nations people and environmental groups joined by Pacific Wild have launched a major campaign. The Canadian provincial and national governments appear gridlocked. In any event the controversy will in all probability last for years. For more information see www.pacificwild.org.

While the rainforest is a wilderness vacation destination for most of us, for many people it is home. The Heiltsuk, Heisla, Oweekeno, and Nuxalk First Nations have made their home here for generations. Archeological excavations at Namu show it has been occupied for at least 9,000 years.

The Koeye River is five miles south of Namu. It is unusual among the watersheds on the Inside Passage in that the river dumps directly into Fitz Hugh Sound instead of emptying into a vast estuary at the head of a deep inlet. The Koeye River is in the center of the traditional home of the Heiltsuk people, and has been vital to their culture for centuries. Several years ago, land at the mouth of the river, owned by outsiders, was clearcut and a fishing lodge built. By that time the sport fishing had collapsed, however, and the lodge never officially opened. Then Karen and Ian raised funds to buy the property and deeded it to the Heilsuk people. It served as a summer camp for children and a guest lodge for visitors until it burned a few years ago. It is now being rebuilt.

After leaving Penrose Island and before turning west into Lama Passage, you enter the more protected waters of Fitzhugh Sound, a good place to spot both orcas and humpbacks. One summer day I watched a young humpback swim along side of *Sundown*. When the youngster got too close, its mother would move between it and the boat and push it a bit away. It was obvious that neither whale was bothered by our boat and that the mother was using us as a teaching aid.

From Fitzhugh Sound, the usual route through Lama passage leads to a good anchorage in Lizzie Cove. From Lizzie Cove it is just an hour to Bella Bella and Shearwater.

Bella Bella is a thriving First Nations village and the center of modern Heiltsuk culture. There is a grocery store, liquor store, fuel dock, medical facility, and many friendly people. Shearwater, a white settlement, is just around the corner. A motel, grocery store, restaurant, fuel dock, repair facilities, and marine store make this a welcome stopover for boaters. It's a good idea to stock up in Bella Bella and Shearwater because the next opportunity, Prince Rupert, lies 195 miles to the north. It is a beautiful 195 miles passing Milbank Sound, Klemtu, Cougar Bay, Grenville Channel, Union Passage, Buttedale, Lowe Inlet, Klewnuggit Inlet, Baker Inlet and Kumealon Inlet. After that British Columbia is behind us and Alaska is ahead.

11 PAINTING OUT THE MORTGAGE STRIPE

It was a grand and glorious day. The sun was shining, the birds were singing and spring was in the air. Well, at least it wasn't raining at the moment. This is, after all, the Northwest. And it was the day for painting out the mortgage stripe. The bank no longer owned any piece of my boat. The mortgage had been paid off and I owned her free and clear, lock, stock and barrel.

Well, maybe. After all, *Sundown* had been built in Canada. And although she was now documented by the United States Coast Guard and had been certified by the United States Congress for commercial work, it was not entirely clear to me that she was in fact all mine. In the old days, in England and her colonies—I begin again—within the British Commonwealth, it was at one time the case, so I have been told, that the Crown retained one sixteenth ownership in every vessel. The purpose of this provision was to permit the legal confiscation of any boat needed in time of war. You've just got to watch the British every step of the way.

Actually, I really didn't think that in 1993 the British navy would have had much use for *Sundown*.

As I was saying, in the old days of abundant salmon and active

95

fisheries up and down the Northwest coast, with salmon canneries in almost every town and port, most of the seiners were owned by the fisheries companies: Nel Bro, Canadian Fisheries, Alaskan Seafood, and the others. Each of these companies adopted a distinctive primary color and identified their boats by painting a recessed stripe along the side. That way, a skipper could tell who were his friends and who his enemies. Moreover, each fishing season, a certain portion of the skipper's pay was applied to his equity in the boat. In a good fishing year, the skipper bought more of the boat; in a lean year, less. In most cases, it took double digit years to pay off the company and to own one's own boat. However, when that did happen, it was a proud and happy day for the skipper, his family and his fishing buddies. They gathered, consumed beverages, and painted out the mortgage stripe. Frequently these proud boats were passed down from father, to son, to grandson, and they continued to fish the cold waters of the Northwest.

So, recognizing the significance of tradition, we also gathered, consumed beverages, and proceeded with the ceremony of painting out the mortgage stripe. Finally, I owned *Sundown*.

Over the next few years I got to know *Sundown* pretty well. I knew much of her planking because I watched as expert shipwrights replaced water-soaked planks. I began to understand her mechanical systems. I discovered ancient bits of her history as I looked into, behind, and under various lockers. I learned many of her eccentricities, including when to clean the furnace, how to use compressed air to blow out the oil supply line to the galley range, how to manage her rigging and stop her leaks.

One summer, as I headed north, I radioed ahead to friends that we were on my way. Over the radio, I heard Susie call out to her partner, "Buddy, *Sundown* is coming and she's bringing

Joseph." A realization that had been growing deep within me suddenly came to the surface: I really did not own *Sundown* after all. I was only her temporary caretaker and guardian. *Sundown* had been traveling the Northwest waters since 1924. I was a new-comer.

Sundown was built before I was born. Long before I discovered the Pacific Northwest, she had explored the waterways of the Inside Passage. In her navigation locker were charts fifty years old with pencil drawn headings, charted by her previous skipper, Capt. Bowles, who had skippered her for almost thirty years. Her planking of yellow cedar came from ancient Northwest trees. Dozens of workers had built her, maintained her, cared for her. She was known in villages and ports all around Vancouver Island and she appeared in books about fishing and logging in the Northwest. She was a tradition; I was a newcomer.

I sold *Sundown* ten years ago; passed her on to another skipper's care. But obviously I haven't let her go. Unfortunately her new owner did. He lost the thread. He didn't understand the tradition. Today she lies sadly at the dock, unused, and unappreciated, in need of paint, repairs and love. I guess traditions have their value and I guess they sometimes come to an end. Nevertheless, I have been tempted, in the dark of night, to take brush and paint bucket to the dock *Sundown* no longer leaves, and paint back in her mortgage stripe.

12 THE LAND OF THE SPIRIT BEAR: BELLA BELLA TO PRINCE RUPERT

Bella Bella to Cougar Bay--47 miles
Cougar Bay to Lowe Inlet--83 miles
Lowe Inlet to Prince Rupert--60 miles

Bella Bella is about half way to Ketchikan. That could be nearly half way or only half way; depends on whether your cup is half full or half empty, and on the weather. Some years the weather is delightful and one year it rained every day but six. We begin to realize how far we have come, and how far we have to go; and we anticipate how long the return trip will be. There is no way around the fact: the Inside Passage is a long, hard trip. It is also one of the great lifetime experiences.

After leaving Vancouver Island, the mainland coast seems a remote, isolated wilderness. You are pretty much on your own except for float planes and the ferry between Port Hardy, Bella Bella, and Prince Rupert. With our usual touchstones of civilization and security receding, it is easy to become disoriented, or rather, oriented to a different compass and a different perspective. Slowly, however, the life of the Central Coast begins to

UNITED STATES ALASKA
CANADA BRITISH COLUMBIA
Dixon Entrance

Brundige Inlet

■ **Prince Rupert**

Lowe Inlet

Hecate Strait

Gil Island

Cougar Bay

**Haida
Gwaii**

Bella Bella

Scale in Miles

N

0 10 20 30 40 50   100

reveal itself. About half of the 5000 residents of the Central Coast belong to First Nations, and the presence of their cultures begins to emerge. The richness of the natural environment also asserts itself. Cultural and environmental issues become much more evident. The threats of environmental destruction and cultural colonialism become tangible and compelling.

At first my goal was Alaska and the destination obscured the journey. Leaving Bella Bella, I pushed toward Prince Rupert, thinking the intervening water to be a wilderness, sparsely inhabited, undeveloped and uninteresting. I was mistaken. When I slowed down, I found a magic space vibrant with life, adventure and rich rewards.

When I first traveled the Inside Passage, there were no comprehensive cruising guides. I had Walt Woodward's delightful and helpful book, How to Cruise to Alaska Without Rocking the Boat Too Much, and the US and Canadian Coast Pilots, but they left a lot of questions unanswered. Now there are the wonderful guides by Don Douglass & Reanne Hemingway-Douglass, as well as the Waggoner Cruising Guide and Northwest Boat Travel. But these guides were not available then. I took a roll of charts down to Squalicum Harbor in Bellingham, and a helpful fisherman drew the route on them with a pencil. Besides those few charts I had dividers and parallels, a depth sounder and a compass. That was about it. Except for the warning, "Don't stop at Klemtu." I got this message repeatedly: "Avoid Klemtu." "Klemtu is dangerous." "The natives are not friendly in Klemtu." My own experience reinforced the advice. Once we anchored about five miles from the village and stayed awake most of the night as loud outboards roared past close enough to rock the boat. Were we in danger of being boarded or was that only our imagination? Whatever, we got the message. We were not welcome in Klemtu.

That was a long time ago. Now Klentu has a website. All things change. In 1996 the first passenger ferry in 19 years stopped at Klemtu. About the same time, the tribal council voted the village dry. Now there is a big welcome sign on the dock and Klemtu is busy attracting the tourist trade. It is the destination for people from all over the world who come seeking the Spirit Bear. Klemtu, like other native villages and towns on the Inside Passage, and like developing countries all over the world, is trying to figure out how to utilize the advantages of modernization while avoiding the disadvantages of western secularization.

Throughout the Inside Passage and in the not too distant past, logging companies gained access to First Nations resources with the promise of jobs and economic gain. The promises seldom materialized, and after the trees were gone, the local people were much as before--only now without their trees. Indiscriminate and greedy logging and fishing have destroyed entire ecosystems, including the people who were dependent on them. After destroy-ing a balance that had been reached over thousands of years, the industries destroyed themselves because they consumed the resource that sustained them. Fishing and logging have given way to fish farms and tourism, and the self-destructive cycle threatens to repeat itself. Fish farms have proven to be terribly destructive to native salmon and marine environments and contribute little to the local economy, filling only the pockets of their absentee landlords. Tourists bring much needed money, but they also bring pollution and an incompatible culture of consumerism and exploitation. The Northwest is following Riverside, California, where the orange groves have been cut down to provide parking spaces for the tourists who come to see the orange groves. In

Skagway, Alaska, the old buildings have been replaced with replicas of what tourists think Alaskan towns should look like. In Sitka and Ketchikan instead of shops offering indigenous goods, tourists can buy Rolex watches and fur coats from stores owned by the cruise lines, and they can see re-enactments of aboriginal ceremonies produced for the tourist market, but containing no heart or soul. The result is a vicious circle with everyone feeling victimized by artificiality and exploited for corporate profit.

North of Bella Bella, before Klemtu, I visit a remote and peaceful anchorage of special beauty and magic. Approaching the anchorage I enter a narrow passage, and pass close to a cliff rising straight from the water. Above me, the cliff shelters an ancient burial site. I was told that long ago a respected chief buried his daughter here. Nestled on a narrow ledge and marked by subtle orange pictographs, the site retains an air of dignity and mystery. Not far away I anchor near the remains of a fish trap, evidence of regular occupation long ago. The fish trap is a ridge of rocks laid between high and low tide levels at the mouth of a small stream. Salmon enter at high tide, head up the stream to spawning beds, and at low tide find themselves trapped. If you want fish, it sure beats dragging a line behind the boat hoping some salmon will mistake the lure for a herring.

Near the north point of the anchorage, I visit the ruins of an ancient big house. Although the house was set back a bit from the shore, its location near the point provided good observation of approaches from any direction. Now the ruins are almost indistinguishable from the undergrowth; each time I must search them out again. One massive door post still stands, but the others are lying in the heavy moss, slowly returning to the rainforest soil from which they came. It is hardly a tourist attraction--just some old logs with faint remains of carvings. But there is something haunting, eerie, and compelling about sitting there in the soft moss, letting my roaming thoughts and complex emotions swirl around a way of life in tune with the changing cycles of nature rather than one obsessed with permanence and security.

Larry Jorgenson from Bella Bella introduced me to some of the history and culture of this area. While his birth family is European, Larry has lived most of his life on the Central Coast and is a powerful spokesman for Heiltsuk culture and homeland. Currently Larry coordinates the visitor program at a Lodge on the Koeye River. Failing to visit this unique facility is to miss an exceedingly rare and moving experience. The day we first met Larry he gave us a personal and graphic introduction to the cultural history of the region. We beached the skiff and Larry asked us to stay behind as he walked into the forest. In the guttural Heiltsuk language he called to the spirit of the ancients, asking permission to enter their homeland. Shortly he returned and guided us quietly through the wet, rich undergrowth. He showed us petroglyphs, pictographs, and culturally modified trees, all quiet but powerful evidence of long and continuous occupation.

After leaving Bella Bella the way leads north past Saunders Island and Dryad Point Light and then west into Seaforth Channel. The navigational aids at Regatta Rocks and Dall Rocks can be confusing, but the chart symbol of a ship wreck at that site is sufficient inducement to sort them out.

Then there is Milbank Sound. Milbank is another of the areas exposed to open ocean swells. The configuration of the coastline and islands can produce extraordinarily unpleasant sea conditions. In the past there was no alternative but to round Ivory Island Light and head across the Sound, a short, but frequently uncomfortable crossing. Now however, with Nobeltec on watch, I turn north just inside Ivory Island and take Ried Passage to Lake Island and Mathieson Channel. This route has its obstacles and would otherwise be impossible without local knowledge, but now it's a piece of cake.

Our destination is Cougar Bay, just beyond the picturesque lighthouse at Boat Bluff and 10 miles north of Klemtu. It's best to anchor just inside the hook on the starboard side entering the bay, although the head of the bay also provides good holding ground. Cougar Bay is on Princess Royal Island, the home of the Spirit Bear. I've seen these elusive and fascinating animals at the mouth of the Canoona River, walking the beach, turning over rocks, looking for seafood snacks. Since the Canoona dumps directly into Graham Reach there is no anchorage. Unless someone stays aboard on watch while the shore party explores up toward Canoona Lake, the best option is to anchor in Green Inlet and take a skiff over to the Canoona. An even better option is to hire a local guide from Hartley Bay. Once, I stayed on *Sundown* in Graham Reach while a shore party went exploring. As they unpacked their gear on the rocks, a spirit bear watched from just inside the bushes, then slowly rambled off through the trees. That day, the watch party had more fun than the shore party. We saw the bear; the bear saw them; but they missed the whole show.

To the east, the Green, Khutz, and Altanhash Inlets reach deep into the coastal range. Not many mariners go there because the anchorages are deep and tricky. But the rewards are huge. More than once I've come back from a skiff trip up one of these rivers with the prop torn to shreds by the rocky bottom. But the chance of seeing spawning salmon, eagles, and grizzly bears more than compensates for the prop.

Just to the north, Wright Sound is where the fool catcher caught the 400 foot ferry, *Queen of the North*, sinking her in a thousand feet of water. How could this happen? How could the flag ship of the British Columbia ferry system, with all the latest electronic navigation aids, hit an island?

I blame the fool catcher. He is out there most often at night and when the weather and sea are rough. He usually strikes after several gaps in attention, none of which individually would have been disastrous. Night is for sleeping, but when I do run in the dark or fog, I have all the help I can get on the bridge: two radars, two GPS systems, and at least two people on watch. The price of floatability is redundancy. So far, so good; the fool catcher hasn't got me yet, but I hope I never forget how close he is.

It's an old story that trouble comes in threes. My own rule of thumb is, if something isn't working properly, fix it now. Otherwise, something else will not be working and then a third, and then a mess. I think this is the best reason for having a routine of raising and lowering flags and other seemingly unnecessary activities. It keeps us on watch for the fool catcher. I also follow the rule of three when navigating: three independent sources of information: visual, radar, and GPS. If all three don't agree, I stop and figure it out. Two out of three is not good enough.

It was the heroic people from the First Nations village at Hartley Bay, seven miles to the north of Gill Island, who came to the rescue of the passengers on the *Queen of the North*. I experienced their generosity of spirit myself when I visited this small village several years ago. Dock space for visitors was limited, but the friendliness and helpfulness of the people appeared boundless. They found a way to fit us in. As I walked up the short dock that first time, a man and woman were cleaning freshly caught Coho salmon on the walkway. I watched for a few minutes and then the man asked, "Would you like a fish?" Remembering my cross-cultural lessons about the importance of giving in native cultures, I responded that I would. He told me to pick one. I chose a beautiful, eight pound, iridescent Silver salmon. That evening, smoked over alder on the back deck, it was one of the best I've ever eaten, the taste certainly improved by the spirit of giving.

I returned to Hartley Bay several years later to pick up Marvin Robinson, a member of the Gitga'at band, and a skilled guide. *Sundown* was accompanying *Explorer*, out of Bellingham, skippered by Richard Friedman, on an expedition in search of the Spirit Bear and information on spawning salmon. The expedition was organized by "OneWorldJourneys.com." (Their website is adventure city for the armchair traveler. Go to www.oneworldjourneys.com; click on Expeditions; click on Salmon.) We had been in Prince Rupert for a week of torrential rain, but the day the rain broke, *Explorer* arrived and we headed south. We picked up Marvin in Hartley Bay and made for anchorage at the head of Khutze Inlet. The next day photographers, videographers, writers, and support team went up river, and I watched, fascinated, as the One World Journeys' crew donned wetsuits so they could lie in the stream to photograph the spawning salmon. I returned to *Sundown* with a once-in-a-lifetime experience and a skiff prop ground to a nubbin in the shallow river. The next day the film crew went to the Canoona and watched black bears, but no Spirit Bear. That evening, pictures and text were uploaded to the One World Journeys website via satellite and we sat around the dinner table discussing questions and comments that people back in civilization had sent in response to the previous day's work. That evening two humpbacks came into the inlet. Very spooky hearing them blow close to the boat in an otherwise still and quiet inlet.

Each year as Sainty Point came abeam and I entered Grenville Channel, I began to look for *Princeton I*, Dave Lewis's proud old wooden patrol boat with her marvelous Gardner Diesel. I knew Dave would be around somewhere or someone would tell me he had headed back to Rupert for a few days. Dave was a civilian fisheries patrol officer for the Canadian Department of Fisheries. Unlike the US, where the fishing fleet is patrolled by law enforcement officers, Canada contracts with civilians to assure compliance by commercial fishermen. Actually, there really isn't much monitoring to do; just knowing someone is about is sufficient to encourage fair play by the fishermen.

One year Dave radioed that he was in Union Passage and encouraged me to join him for the evening. Union Passage is entered through Hawkins Narrows, and on my chart the Narrows looked to be about three feet deep and six feet wide. Even though I knew Dave was a super cautious mariner and that he was familiar with *Sundown*, my natural caution (read fear of grounding) won out. "No way," I said, "I can't get through there." "Oh come on, Joseph" Dave responded, "there is plenty of water." I just couldn't go there. So Dave got in his skiff and came out into Grenville Channel to lead me in to a beautiful and peaceful anchorage. We rafted to *Princeton I* and had a delightful evening of food, drink, and talk.

I had met Dave years earlier in Lowe Inlet. Lowe has always been a special place for me. Not only is it beautiful, Lowe is a failsafe anchorage, easy to find, safe to enter, large enough to swing at anchor, excellent holding ground, and secure in any weather. The only problem is the mosquitoes. Because Lowe is so well protected from wind and the water is so calm, not only do mariners love it, so do the mosquitoes. As I entered Lowe that first year, *Princeton I* immediately caught my attention. A classic British Columbia patrol boat, her lines were fair and her demeanor appealing. I was puzzled, however, that she was not in the main anchorage, but off to the side and in the current from Verney Falls. A person whom I assumed to be her skipper was watching *Sundown* as we set our anchor. I rowed over to *Princeton I*, and thus began a friendship with Dave that has continued to the present. Dave has been not only my friend, but my mentor. One year he took me on a magnificent tour of the Skenna River, with its world-famous, nutrient rich Sockeye salmon. Dave explained that during the second world war the US Defense Department determined that these particular Sockeye had the highest oil content and the highest nutritional value of any salmon. Skeena River Sockeye fed many soldiers around the world. On that first meeting, I learned from Dave that by anchoring where she did, *Princeton I* rode steady in the gentle current and the slight movement of the water kept the mosquitoes away. Only a hundred yards from the main anchorage, Dave knew how to make his stay exceedingly more comfortable. Never underestimate local knowledge.

Lowe is entered between James Point and Hepburn Point. Past Whiting Bank, one keeps to starboard at Don Point to avoid the rock mid channel. Pass Pike Point and Mark Bluff; then enter Nettle basin. The inner anchorage is dominated by a grand cascade: Verney Falls. If my timing is good the Sockeye that spawn in the lakes above the cascade are returning. There is a trail on the north side of the falls that leads out onto the edge of the cascade. Sitting there on the rocks, I watch the beautiful Sockeye battle the torrent of water as they struggle to reach their spawning grounds.

I had seen pictures and movies of salmon returning from the ocean to their stream of origin. But nothing can convey the power of the experience of being close enough to touch them as they fight the falls. Their struggle is truly a battle to the death. They do not simply wiggle their tails and swim upstream against the surging water. I watch a particular fish. It lunges upwards, falls back, lunges again, falls back, over and over. Finally, there is a subtle change in the water, or the fish moves in an imperceptibly different way and it reaches the safety of an eddy behind a bolder. It rests for a couple of minutes and then attempts the next hurdle--and fails. It is washed down to the bottom of the falls. The advance it had gained is lost. Almost immediately it lunges up again, and the struggle is repeated. Finally it again achieves the eddy behind the boulder. Then, into the current again and this time it succeeds. It reaches the next resting pool. In the course of an hour I see this battle repeated dozens of times. And I see perhaps twenty fish that finally make it through the cascades to the relative calm of Kumowdah River above. Hundreds more remain stranded beneath the falls.

Only the strongest conquer the falls and spawn. Thus natural selection insures the survival of the species. Not so for hatchery fish.

Year after year the salmon return to spawn and die. Their carcasses fertilize the forests, estuaries and inlets. Year after year the smolt begin their four-year journey to the open Pacific, and year after year they return to battle the falls. I am overwhelmed by the power of this life-force, this will to survive and procreate. The forces of death are strong: storms wash away the eggs in the winter; predators eat the fry on their way downstream in the spring. After four years in the open ocean, the salmon face orcas, eagles, bears, wolves and fishermen as they seek to return not only to their own original stream, but also to the exact spawning ground where they hatched. The female wears away her tail to bare raw bone as she digs her redd, making a nest in the gravel for her eggs. After rejecting various suitors, she selects a mate. A brief courting ritual follows and she expels hundreds of eggs that he covers with sperm.

She covers the fertilized eggs with gravel. Then, exhausted by the struggle to reach the spawning grounds and by the efforts of mating, they give themselves to the current and are washed downstream to die and fertilize the forest and ocean. The story has been told many times, but the power of life to overcome the forces of death becomes real for me as I watch the saga of one salmon trying again and again to conquer the power of the water at Verney Falls.

Not only is the passage to Alaska long, it is also expensive. So I started a charter business. "Eco-adventure Cruises," the literature read. "Experience the legendary Northwest aboard a Northwest Legend." I had some grand adventures and met some wonderful people. My advice to anyone thinking about starting a charter business? Don't go there. It was, nevertheless, one of the happiest times of my life.

During the first three years of charters we had many days on the water without customers. So I offered free charters to environmental and non-profit groups. They paid only for food, drink and fuel. It was a good idea. Not only were we making a contribution to environmental protection, we were getting good publicity and having a good time. One summer we hosted a team from the Sierra Club. Another year, Doug Peacock was aboard and wrote about his experience for the Natural Resources Defense Council.

Doug was a close friend of Edward Abbey, and is one of the three people alive who know where Abbey is buried--alone in the desert where he wanted to be. Doug was the model for Abbey's character, Heyduke, and while on *Sundown*, Doug lived up to his legacy.

Doug Peacock was a magnificent guest and I would have him on board anytime, but I began to realize that all people concerned about our environment are not alike. I began to wonder if offering free charters to environmental groups was such a good idea after all. There are environmentalists and there are environmentalists. I learned that the people who paid for their trips were most appreciative, and that often as not environmentalists were blinded by their ideology not only to the environment, but also to the people around them. There were days when we traveled through some of the most magnificent water on the globe while the environmentalists hunched over charts arguing among themselves about this or that. They did not experience the environment, nor did they learn from people who knew it intimately.

Previously I had divided things up pretty simply and neatly: there were the environmentalists and there were the developers. One group wore white hats and Birkenstocks and were the good guys and the other group wore black hats and ties and were the bad guys. Slowly it began to dawn on me that this western movie mentality wasn't working. I began to realize that there is not much difference between a doctrinaire environmentalist and a doctrinaire developer.

What will save our planet will not be the people who are dedicated to a cause, but people who are able to think outside the box, develop alliances with other open-minded people, and forge new visions of a complex future--people like Edward Abbey and Doug Peacock. It was Abbey who wrote, "Growth is the enemy of progress."

At its north end, past Klewnugget Inlet, Baker Inlet, and Kumealon Inlet, Grenville Channel opens into Chatham Sound, the entry to Prince Rupert. From Watson Rock to Lucy Island, Chatham Sound is littered with islands, rocks, and navigational aids. And since Prince Rupert is a major port, there is heavy freighter traffic. When the Skeena River Sockeye are running, gillnetters fill the sound. The fishermen, freighters, rocks, islands, and navigational aids make Chatham Sound a challenge in the dark or fog. I went through this obstacle course once with only radar to guide me and I will not do that again.

Prince Rupert is the only mainland deep water port in British Columbia north of Vancouver. It is the terminus of the major rail line through northern British Columbia and is the shipping port for timber, fish, coal and other commodities. But since the timber and fish are almost gone, shipping has plummeted. Prince Rupert struggles to find a new identity. It is still a city, however, with a highway to Terrace and the rest of the mainland. There is an airport and also good supermarkets and repair facilities. On the way south, it is necessary to stop in Prince Rupert to clear customs, so, heading north, unless I need repairs or provisions, I usually pass Prince Rupert and head for Brundige Inlet, the best departure point for crossing Dixon Entrance and entering Alaska.

If you do stop in Prince Rupert, the Prince Rupert Rowing and Yacht Club is the best place to tie up.

The way out of Prince Rupert headed north is through Venn Passage and past the First Nations' settlement of Metlakatla. This route is not for the faint of heart and should be attempted the first time--maybe anytime--only in daylight and good weather. Fifteen navigational aids, one range and three directional lights define the channel and on the way north the range and directional lights must be run looking in the rearview mirror. Several openings that appear to offer good passage are dangerously shallow. Heavy local traffic adds to the fun. Emerging from Venn Passage, it is possible to turn north past Doolan Point, but I always go south around Tugwell Island.

A less challenging route out of Prince Rupert is to re-trace the route south around Digby Island. Once into Chatham Sound, which can be uncomfortably choppy, it is only 26 miles to Brundige Anchorage. Brundige Inlet is safe in all weather and we wait there, frequently with mosquitoes, for good weather to cross Dixon Entrance in the morning.

Dixon Entrance is another transition point. Entering Alaska, everything changes.

13 ALASKA OR BUST: PRINCE RUPERT TO KETCHIKAN

Prince Rupert to Brundige Inlet--33 miles

Brundige Inlet to Foggy Bay--27 miles

Foggy Bay to Ketchikan--35 miles

Over nine hundred miles from Seattle with Alaska now in sight, the true picture of the Inside Passage begins to emerge. This is not only a boat trip across international borders and through countless islands and passages, it is also a deeply personal experience, an intimate challenge to our usual predictable and sanitized lives. Most of our experiences are pre-packaged and mediated by culture, convention, and convenience. We work, play, take care of our responsibilities and families on someone else's schedule and we dance to someone else's music. We escape boredom and frustration by shifting to another schedule, but still not our own. We go on vacation; we become tourists. We go on orchestrated "tours of the wine country," we get life like fast food: standardized and shrink wrapped with preservatives. We drive on the right-hand side of the road, stop at red lights, and listen to the five o'clock news. We are always observing, and observing someone's else's

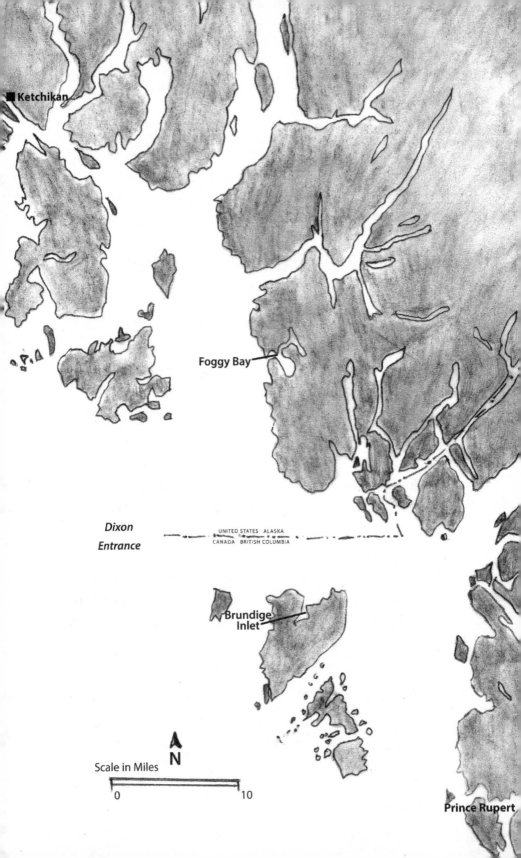

■ Ketchikan

Foggy Bay

Dixon

Entrance

UNITED STATES ALASKA
CANADA BRITISH COLUMBIA

Brundige
Inlet

Scale in Miles

N

0   10

Prince Rupert

interpretation of what they think it is we want to experience.

The opportunities to chart our own course are rare. The Inside Passage is one of those rare experiences. Never mind the cruising guides, GPS, VHF, radar, electronic charts, auto pilot, and cell phones. We crossed Georgia Strait, traveled Malispina Strait, made it through Yuculta Rapids, Green Rapids, Dent Rapids, Wellbore Rapids, up Johnston Strait across Queen Charlotte Strait, past Milbank Sound and Ivory Island Light, Finlayson Sound, Wright Sound, Grenville Channel, Chatham Sound, Dixon Entrance. I damn well drove my own boat to Alaska. As the skipper of *Kay II*, Fred C. Clark, said to me many years ago, "After you've been to Alaska, you walk tall." It is still true.

I was "walking tall" one year in Ketchikan, after having just arrived in *Shadow* with her hot showers, comfortable bed, electronic charts, and hydraulic stabilizers when I ran into a couple I had seen earlier in the year in the San Juans. They had also just arrived. The had paddled all the way in kayaks! Tell me about walking tall? It's all relative.

Dixon Entrance, between Prince Rupert and Ketchikan, marks the international boundary between Canada and the United States; it also is one of the major natural transition zones of the Inside Passage. Like Georgia Strait, the Yuculta Rapids, and Queen Charlotte Strait, Dixon Entrance is a place of change. No longer protected by the sheltered waters of the Great Bear Rain Forest we now confront the open waters and high mountains of Southeast Alaska.

Crossing the border between British Columbia and Alaska is not quite like crossing the Equator; it does, nevertheless, have its effect. As you look north, the high mountains of Alaska dominate the horizon. After the protected waters of the Great Bear Rainforest, the waterways in Alaska seem exposed. It is still inside water, but the distances are greater, the mountains higher, the passages wider. The country is more open and wild. As I cross the border, that imaginary line in the middle of Dixon Entrance, various and conflicting emotions surface. There is exhilaration and relief at having finally made it to Alaska without a disaster. The new territory is both familiar because I am back in US waters and strange because it is Alaska.

Since it is open to the Pacific Ocean, Dixon Entrance can be rough. A very early start from Prince Rupert may work, but Brundige is a much better launching platform.

Leaving Brundige, the choice is where to aim. The closest place across Dixon Entrance is one of the anchorages around Nakat Bay. The problem with that is you still have to get around Cape Fox, so, unless we are just totally wiped out by rough seas, I head for Foggy Bay. If the sea and weather are OK, it's on to Ketchikan. There are other anchorages, but once in the protection of Duke Island, might as well go to town.

Ketchikan lies half-way up Tongass Narrows. Just south of town the channel makes a slight dog leg between California Rock and Idaho Rock. One year, headed south, we left Ketchikan before daylight, hoping to cross Dixon Entrance in the morning calm. At 0600 the cruise liner *Nieuw Amsterdam*, pride of the Holland-American Line and 704 feet long, broadcast her routine security message as she entered Tongass Narrows from Nichols Passage. Since it looked like we would meet *Nieuw Amsterdam* in the dog leg and because there was some morning fog, I responded with our location, course, and speed. *Nieuw Amsterdam* replied asking about our visibility. I answered that visibility was about two miles and asked about conditions at her location. She replied that visibility was zero. At 0610 *Nieuw Amsterdam* was on the radio again; this time to the Ketchikan Coast Guard. She had run aground on Gravina Point and requested deployment of all available Coast Guard boats and oil containment equipment.

On *Sundown* we were just finishing our first cup of coffee and already the day was shaping up. Our alarm at the thought of a major disaster was accompanied by fascination at being on the scene. We were eager to get across Dixon Entrance to Prince Rupert before the wind picked up, but we were intrigued by the unfolding drama. Radio exchanges between *Nieuw Amsterdam* and the coast guard crackled. *Nieuw Amsterdam* retreated to the relative protection of the Blank Islands and was holding her position. The Coast Guard was mobilizing equipment and the Commander was being summoned to the communication center. On *Nieuw Amsterdam*, hull inspections were underway and the Captain was on his way to the bridge. Back and forth, back and forth, there was seldom a gap in radio talk. *Nieuw Amsterdam* did not believe she was in immediate danger and was not lowering her life boats. Preparations were being made for divers to inspect the hull underwater.

Sundown was the only other boat in the vicinity. *Nieuw Amsterdam* carried 1281 passengers and a crew of 500, so what help could we be? Nevertheless we reported our position to the Coast Guard and we were requested to proceed to within visual distance of the *Nieuw Amsterdam* and stand by. The fog was now very thick so in addition to our running lights, we turned on our deck lights, cabin lights and anchor lights and headed out Nichols Passage on the slow bell. Now *Sundown* asserted her own mind and complaining that we had overloaded her electrical system, she tripped her main breaker and shut down all electrical systems. I thought that neither the Coast Guard nor the *Nieuw Amsterdam* would really care about our own problem at this time, so I shifted to neutral, turned off some lights and the coffee pot, and got things fired up again. Soon, the seven hundred foot ocean liner emerged from the fog with awe-inspiring suddenness.

During a lull in the radio traffic a calm voice from the Native village on Annette Island informed the Coast Guard that they had about forty fishing vessels on alert and ready to respond if needed. About the same time, a small high-speed aluminum boat passed us and came alongside *Nieuw Amsterdam*, then quickly pulled away and roared off into the fog. We learned later that the boat was picking up the harbor pilots and taking them back home to Ketchikan. By this time, three tugs were on the scene, so we asked the Coast Guard if we could stand down and that being granted, we headed again for Prince Rupert.

Still excited by the morning adventure we continued to monitor the radio exchanges. The Captain of the *Nieuw Amsterdam* was on the bridge and the Coast Guard Commander was in the office. The Captain determined that while the hull had been holed near the bow, the damage was limited to a relatively small water-tight compartment. There was a 150-200 foot dent in the hull and the port prop was damaged and had leaked a small quantity of hydraulic fluid. The Captain requested permission to continue on to Prince Rupert. The Commander denied permission. The Captain requested permission to return to Ketchikan. The Commander denied permission, but as a precaution had cleared 1000 feet of dock space in Ketchikan. The Commander requested all bridge personnel to be available for an investigation team that was on their way to the site. The Captain responded that the personnel would be available, but had been instructed not to answer any questions until the owner's representative arrived. He was already en route by charter jet from Vancouver. And so the morning's radio drama continued, all the players assuming their roles. What could have been a horrible disaster at sea was morphing into a manageable distraction.

How could a 704 foot modern cruise liner with the latest navigational gear hit an island? According to the Coast Guard investigation, there had been ten people on the bridge at the time including two pilots, the chief engineer, three mates, and the master. The Coast Guard determined that the accident was caused by poor communication between all these people. In officialese: "inadequate bridge resource management." I call it "operator error." The fool catcher is always out there. I've never been able to understand why the pilots were permitted to leave the ship.

As if we had not had enough excitement for the day, when we headed for Prince Rupert with the fog lifting and the sun promising a delightfully calm crossing, we discovered we had a stowaway. A red-breasted nuthatch was clinging tenaciously to our forestay. Although we set out food and water on the forward hatch and named her "Crew," she did not seem particularly happy to be aboard, and from time to time would leave the ship, only to return after discovering that land was some distance away. Ungratefully, she jumped ship as soon as we got within a few yards of shore on the approach to Prince Rupert.

Five years later *Nieuw Amsterdam* was sold by Carnival Cruise Lines, the parent company of Holland American, and replaced by one of their growing fleet of mega luxury liners. The advent of these huge liners and the growth of the Alaskan cruise industry has transformed much of Southeast Alaska. And like the industries that preceded it--fishing, logging, mining, oil--the cruise industry has been a mixed blessing. It has brought income and recognition, but it has also destroyed the resource it exploits.

The grand and beautiful ocean liners such as the *Nieuw Amsterdam* have been replaced by immense and ugly floating hotels with equally ugly names: *Radiance of the Seas, Celebrity Infinity, Dawn Princess, Sun Princess, Norwegian Star, Norwegian Dream,* and so on. The *Carnival Conquest,* for example, is 952 feet long (over three football fields), has fourteen decks, carries a staff and crew of 1,150, and 2,974 passengers. She cruises at 21 knots and displaces 110,000 tons. Fuel consumption was not reported, neither was the number of toilets. (I wonder if they are called "heads.")

Another liner, the *Crown Princess,* carries 3,080 passengers, has nearly 900 balcony staterooms, an entire deck of mini-suites. She is 952 feet in length, weighs 113,000 gross tons, carries 19 decks, and is registered in Bermuda and Gibraltar. She offers twelve dining rooms and cafes, room service, an outdoor theatre, casino, six swimming pools, nine hole putting course, jogging track, and a "Hearts and Minds" wedding chapel.

Here is a paragraph from one of the websites:

"Many of the ships sailing to Alaska include cabins with the latest trend incruising—private verandahs. Cruisers go to Alaska to see the magnificent mountains, beautiful bays, and wonderful wildlife. How better to see all of this than from your own private balcony? In addition to the verandahs, ships cruising Alaska often include huge observation lounges and heated indoor/outdoor pools. You don't have to "rough it" to see all that Alaska has to offer."

Even the Inside Passage is available pre-packaged and shrink-wrapped from your private veranda and without rough edges. As many as five of these gargantuan vessels can be in a tiny Alaskan port at the same time. They overwhelm the waterfront as they each disgorge two thousand passengers onto shore in Ketchikan, Sitka, Juneau or Skagway. Like a macro version of the observer effect described by quantum mechanics, the presence of the observer has destroyed what was to be seen. The frontier they came to see has been replaced by up-scale shops, frequently owned by the cruise lines selling everything from miniature totem poles made in Korea to oversize fur coats from Siberia. When the Alaska season is over, the shops are closed down and moved to the Caribbean for the cruising season there, selling the same Rolex and de Cardin. Not only is Alaska being exploited, but also the passengers. How can a person get any sense of the last frontier from a "huge observation lounge" and traveling in a group of 2000?

Even with a heated pool.

Before the cruise ships, Ketchikan still retained the rawness and spontaneity of a frontier town. Most visitors found a berth at Thomas Basin just south of the center of town or went north of town to Bar Harbor, but I preferred City Dock in the center of town where the fishermen tied up. It was a noisy, busy, odoriferous place with float planes landing and taking off in the midst of tug boats, seiners, gillnetters, and trollers coming and going. One evening we were in the middle of nine seiners rafted together. Fishermen in all conditions of sobriety clambered over our decks at all hours of the day and night. In the morning we found a salmon, a halibut and a bucket of crabs they had left for us. Rafted in the middle of a bunch of fishing boats may not be ideal for a yachting vacation, but it does have its compensations.

Nearby on Water Street I found a small shop that specialized in everything: artifacts from the Klondike, old brass boat stuff, antiques, junk, chess sets, knives, and guns. It was a wonderful treasure house with nothing useful, but much to be desired. I bought a copy of Cap Hansen's Handbook in almost new condition, a pair of earrings made from halibut ears, some jingle shells, and a pineapple deck prism. Now that store has been replaced by a shop selling Rolex and de Cardin and it's hard to find anyone who even knows what halibut ears are, much less Cap Hansen's Handbook.

Back then the bar in Annabelles still smelled like whiskey, and breakfast at the Roller Bay Café was eggs, sausage, pancakes, biscuits with gravy, and pecan pie. Tongass Hardware on Front Street carried everything a mariner might desire. The Roller Bay and Tongass Hardware are still there, and if you get through the swarms of tourists you can probably find what you are looking for--except the pecan pie. And although Creek Street no longer provides what it was famous for during the gold-rush days, Dollie's house still stands as a reminder of different rhythms, and dozens of people still catch salmon from the Creek Street bridge just across the street.

City Dock is now an immense pier for the cruise liners. Instead of tug boats, fishing boats, and gifts of salmon and crabs, charter boats and tour boats clamor for customers.

While the cruise industry has transformed Southeast, it has also brought some money--the defense of every invasive industry. As I was writing this story I wanted more information on the *Nieuw Amsterdam* grounding so I contacted Terry Miller at the Ketchikan Daily News who remembered the incident and referred me to Debbie Gravel at the Public Library. Debbie also remembered the grounding, researched their archives, and sent me photocopies of articles. She told me that both her husband

and her son work in the cruise ship industry.

Rheba Dupras from Alaska's "Ask a Librarian Service" also searched her archives and sent photo copies.

Terry, Debbie and Rheba seemed genuinely interested in what I was doing, personally eager to help, and reminded me of many other people in Southeast who have gone out of their way to help a Chichaco. (There are two social classes on the last frontier: cheechako who have recently arrived, and sourdoughs who got there first.) That is what I like best about Southeast--the people. They seem more free, happy and helpful than the rest of us.

For example, on my first trip to Alaska, *Raven* developed an alarming vibration in her propulsion system. I was about as lost as I have ever been, somewhere between Juneau and Glacier Bay. According to my limited chart inventory the closest dock was in Excursion Inlet, so I headed there. I tied to a float at a remote fish processing plant and wandered ashore looking for help. I eventually found an office and explained my plight to a man behind a desk. He must have realized how green and pitiful I was because he told me to "go see Karl in the shop and tell him I said fix it." I found the shop and Karl who was right out of a movie set: heavy, cigar smoking, wearing a dirty sleeveless undershirt. When I delivered my message he said he would get to it later. I had no clue what "later" meant, but I had no alternative, so I settled in. That afternoon, Karl hauled *Raven*, found a thrown cutlass bearing, removed the bearing and took it to the office. The next day a new bearing arrived on the company plane from Seattle, Karl installed it and put *Raven* back in the water. They charged me $14 for the bearing. This was the way I found things in Southeast.

Some years later, we arrived in Ketchikan with a yearning for salmon and none in the freezer. The cook headed to the supermarket for fish. She returned with salmon and a story. When she asked for salmon, she was greeted with a smile and something close to incredulity. "We never carry salmon," she was told. "Everyone here catches their own." As the cook's face fell, the butcher said, "I have some frozen King salmon at home in my freezer. If you can wait for a few minutes, I'll go home and get you some." Of course there was no charge. Gifted salmon always tastes special.

So the Inside Passage to Alaska is not only about a fantastic cruise through natural wonders, and a journey of self-discovery; it is also a discovery of the people who still live a frontier mentality and morality and who do not get their experiences shrink wrapped. In spite of cruise liners, oil drilling in the Arctic National Wildlife Refuge, clear cut logging, over fishing, gold mining and every other kind of environmental exploitation, Alaska remains wild and free. And for the most part, so do the people--friendly, open, helpful, wild and free.

14 TENAKEE SLOWS

W e had been told that Tenakee Springs was one of the places we should visit in Southeast Alaska. So, not knowing what else to do our first time in Southeast, we went there. The harbor wasn't much, but in those days a lot of harbors in Southeast weren't much. More often than not, no one seemed to care where you parked your boat or whether or not you paid for moorage. So we found some dock space, tied to the broken bull rail as best we could, and made our way up the muddy path in what we assumed was the direction of the village. Various bits of the past littered the beach--old machinery, broken bicycles, trash, and long abandoned hulks of what had at one time been gillnetters or trollers. One hulk near the dock was years beyond floating: her house caved in, planks sprung loose from a few remaining frames. There was, however one piece of her well maintained and freshly painted: her name board. And the name, reminding us that she was not only a dying hulk, but the embodiment of someone's work and dreams, was--*Don't Worry*.

The woman we met on the path was dressed in what we came to learn was Tenakee formal: gum boots, slicker, old hat. We asked directions, although there was only one path as far as we could see, and plied her with various other questions that she must have been asked by every visitor she had ever encountered. But she answered graciously, with typical Southeast hospitality, and only smiled when we said that we would be leaving that afternoon.

Three days later when we happened to pass her again on the path, her face broke into a happy grin: "Ah ha." she said, "The Tenakee Slows got ya." And they had. We stayed for a week, went to Juneau, and returned for another month to enjoy the clams, crabs, salmon and a community of people that little village fostered.

There were not many tourists or tourist attractions in Tenakee. Sometimes someone opened a restaurant in their home, but you could never be sure where it would be from year to year. There was a library up the trail but it was usually not open. The two old Buddha diesels in the electrical plant could hold your attention only so long. But there were three defining events: the most magnificent hot spring, the general store, and the tide. They all had hours. The hot spring had men's and women's hours. The store was open from time to time. And of course the tides had their own rhythm. So, if you timed your soak, and bought your supplies, the tide was wrong to leave. If you got the tide right, you missed your soak, or the store was closed. It took several days to get all this organized, buy ice, have one last soak, and catch the tide: the inexorable Tenakee Slows at work.

The hot spring was everything. Located in the center of the village, it was housed in one of the few buildings that didn't need paint. Posted on the door were men's and women's hours through the day. Whether there were co-ed hours during the night seemed never to be publicly discussed. The dressing room was clean and neat, with a wood stove. The spring room had a concrete floor and in the center a huge pool of clear, steaming water. You look down and it seemed as if you could see through the water to the center of the earth. There were scoops made from old plastic Clorox bottles and bars of soap. The drill was to dip some hot water, soap up, and rinse off on the concrete before entering the pool.

I was told that the local women brought their children to soak, and that their hours took the place of gossip around the kitchen table. News of the day and of families. Local politics and infidelities. All the conversation that nurtured individuals and the village. Men's hours were somewhat less verbal and usually include a six-pack or two. "Uhh." "Beer?", "Not many fish." "Rain." "Hot." "Uhh." That was about the extent of the masculine vocabulary. But then, it's just the modesty naked men usually feel in the presence of other naked men. Or perhaps there was a connection beyond words.

There were about forty houses in the village, strung along both sides of the dirt path that paralleled the shore, and it was the people who had chosen to make Tenakee their home that provided the richest experiences. Just past the hot spring house, over on the left, the water side, I saw a man bending over a number 3 wash tub. I walked over. And thus began one of the special encounters that make life in Southeast so amazing.

Ryder Converse was cleaning clams. These were not steamers. Each clam was about the size of a tennis ball. We had a nice chat; he showed me how to cut out the stomachs, leaving only the soft, rich flesh, and how to pack them in Mason jars for canning. We agreed to meet at my boat the next morning at low tide when he would take me to dig some clams for my own canning.

The next morning just as the tide turned Ryder appeared with his constant companion, a miniature poodle, Skipper. A short run in Ryder's aluminum outboard, with Skipper in the bow, ears flapping in the wind, we grounded on a small island and soon had a five-gallon bucket full of beautiful tennis ball clams. The clam chowder that evening was outstanding and even better was the chowder we made all winter from clams we dug and canned that day.

Ryder and Skipper were inseparable, as were Ryder and a can of beer. I never saw Ryder drunk or even tipsy; he opened the first beer of the day about the time most of us were having our second cup of morning coffee, and managed a steady equilibrium through the day. I heard that some people called Ryder the unofficial mayor of Tenakee, but to me he was just Ryder.

Ryder was also inseparable from his wife, Vicky. Sometimes, when Vicky needed some space, or wanted to visit their children, she would take the ferry to Juneau. That was fine with Ryder for about two days. That was his limit. Then he was off to Juneau to be with Vicky. Their Tenakee neighbors said it was as predictable as the tides.

We went over to Juneau one day to buy a new compass for *Raven* and Ryder went along. It was a pleasant trip. In between beers Ryder napped. And he napped on the way home. But as we rounded Point Marsden and entered Chatham Strait, the pleasant part of the trip ended. We found ourselves in a thick fog bank, almost no visibility, a compass that had not been adjusted, and no idea where Tenakee might be. I called Ryder out of his dreams. He came to the helm, looked around a bit and pointed into the fog. "Head that way," he said, "What does the compass read?" I told him. "OK," and Ryder was back asleep.

I held the compass course for an hour that seemed like weeks with no idea where we would end up, but when the fog finally lifted we were across the Strait and entering Tenakee Inlet.

Another time, toward the end of the summer, as the days were getting shorter, *Raven* was tied to the dock in Tenakee, the weather was changing. Dinner was over, and we were snug aboard. Outside it was dark and cold and the rain seemed to be coming directly from the glaciers to the north in Glacier Bay. We were very happy to be out of the weather. Then there was a bump on the boat and we heard Ryder's voice. Through the aft companionway poured Ryder, two of his cousins, and Skipper. Slickers were flung aside along with gallons of rain water and soon hot coffee and Jim Beam warmed everyone. The cousins had arrived yesterday for three days and so today, Ryder had "shown them Alaska." They had caught salmon in the salt chuck and trout in the river. They had seen whales, eagles, bears, and wolves. They had collected blackberries and clams. They had soaked in the hot spring and been soaked by Southeast rain. If anyone could "show Alaska" in one day, it was Ryder.

Why do we remember these people, these unique, unforgettable, larger than life people, like Ryder? In a short story called "Family Happiness," Tolstoy wrote that happy families are all alike and unhappy families are unhappy each in its own way. I think he got it backwards. There is a certain sameness about unhappy families and people. Happy people and families, however, are each unique. Each has found his or her own note to play in the larger symphony and they play their note with confidence and clarity.

Ryder was one of those people, and he and Vicky were one of those families. They could not be diagnosed; they did not fit any discernable patterns. And so meeting them was a rare privilege and remembering them is poignant and evocative. The Inside Passage seems to have more than its share of these happy and unique people. That is one of the things that keeps calling us back. They call us out of our defined lives and invite us to discover not only their place and their life, but our own.

A few years ago, small cruise boats began to include Tenakee Springs in their itinerary. The Tenakee town council met and passed a resolution that cruise ship tourism was "incompatible with the community's lifestyle, facilities, and services." The council affirmed that "whatever steps are necessary will be taken to prevent this type of tourism in Tenakee Springs." They contacted the cruise company, but to no avail. The boat arrived, and began to disembark it's dozens of passengers. Whatever stores, shops, or restaurants might have been open suddenly closed, and the passenger were met by Tenakee folks who handed out flyers explaining why the people who lived in Tenakee felt that an invasion from the tourist industry would destroy the unique way of life they had and that the tourists had, infact, come to experience. "Come again," the flyer concluded, "but, please, not in large, organized tours."

We seek out places like Tenakee Springs and people like Ryder because they embody a way of life that we have lost and know deeply, perhaps beneath our conscious knowing, that we want and need. Canned tours may take us out of our ordinary lives, but they give us an unsatisfying alternative. We merely substitute one pre-packaged experience for another. Ryder was not pre-packaged and he could not be diagnosed. He was just uniquely Ryder.

What could be a finer epitaph for any of us? Not that I was this or that or achieved something or something else, but that I was just uniquely me. The wonderful and evocative poet, Mary Oliver, said it: "I don't want to end up simply having visited this world."

15 Hand Troller

In the days when there were more commercial fish boats than yachts in Southeast Alaska harbors, moorage was a casual affair. You just tied up wherever there was empty dock space. Since most of the harbors were small and crowded, you rafted to another boat if there was no open dock, and you also expected to be rafted to. It was considered hospitable and prudent to drop fenders over your exposed topside for a potential rafter. Sometimes there was someone to collect dockage and sometimes not. No big deal except for the fact that fishermen tended to come and go at all hours which made un-rafting sometimes interesting. It was not unusual to wake in the morning to find your boat rafted differently than it was when you went to sleep.

If the municipal docks in Ketchikan, Petersburg, Wrangell, Sitka, Elfin Cove, Hoonah, Meyers Chuck, and Pelican were casual, the most casual was Tenakee Springs. Tenakee is a small village, just a dirt path for a main street, one minimalist general store, a fuel dock that was occasionally open, and an absolutely magnificent community hot spring. The harbor, just east of the village and tucked behind a barely adequate floating breakwater, was intended mainly for the residents and a few seasonal fishing boats. There was no harbor master and no moorage fee. So one afternoon we pulled in, tied *Raven* in an empty slip, and settled on the back deck, anticipating a few days of what we came to know as the "Tenakee Slows"--soaks in the hot spring, picking blackberries, and mainly just doing nothing serious.

Earlier in the season, in Wrangell, we had tied *Raven* near a large and expensive Hatteras and had enjoyed the company of her skipper. So when the same Hatteras pulled in to the slip next to us in Tenakee, we invited the skipper over to join the "Tenakee Slows" with us. "Not now," he said. He was in a hurry, he told us, to sell his fish. And he disappeared up the dock with a couple of nice Kings. Obviously the "Slows" had not caught him yet. I wondered what that was about. Where does one sell sport-caught fish?

He came back a bit later and settled down in a deck chair. "What's that 'selling fish' about?" I asked. "Well," he said, "Kings are bringing $3.75 a pound at the dock this year so those two twenty pounders were worth $150." He explained to me that he had a hand troll permit, so he was a commercial fisherman and could sell the fish he caught.

This was all new information for me, but my education as a commercial hand troller was about to begin.

We were familiar with the graceful commercial trollers with their high spreaders, slowly working as many as a hundred hooks through salmon waters. Their lines were managed by hydraulically powered gurdies and it was a good way of life and an adequate income for many fishermen. Joe Upton's classic book, Alaska Blues, tells the story. But hand trolling was something else. An entry level fishery, hand trolling was a way someone with a small boat and limited capital could begin their career. The "hand" part meant that the power driven gear of larger commercial salmon trollers could not be used, only manual gurdies. The Hatteras skipper was just taking advantage of the opportunity. He used his sport fishing gear with some minor additions, caught as many fish as he was able, and sold them at the end of the day. It sounded like a great combination with all the fishing a person could want, no catch limits, and getting paid for it.

Tenakee Slows receded into the background and the next morning we headed for Juneau to buy a license, which at that time cost $20. I found a large chandlery and showed the salesman my brand new license. "I'm a hand troller," I said proudly, "What do I need?" Evidently I was not the first Chichaco the salesman had initiated into the guild of the hand trollers, so with great patience he explained the gear and how a hand troller fished and soon I left the store with snubbers, nylon line, crimpers, flashers, strip holders, frozen herring, and various other bits and pieces of gear. The fun was about to begin.

I learned what it meant to "fish or cut bait." We used herring strips for bait, and these strips we made by filleting herring and carefully trimming the fillets into strips. If there were any ragged edges, the strips would soon tear apart as they were dragged through the water. So it took a sharp knife and steady hand to prepare dozens of strips for the next day's fishing. Gear also had to be prepared. Snubbers and snap swivels attached to one hundred pound test monofilament with lead crimps, flashers polished, strip clips attached.

While "real" hand trollers fished from small commercial vessels and sometimes fished several dozen hooks, we used our light-weight sport downriggers. Every six feet above the 15 pound weight we attached a twelve-foot line with snubber, flasher, and herring strip. We could run six hooks on each side without getting things too tangled up. Then we would also trail one or two rigs on rod and reel in the center, behind the boat.

When a fish struck, the experienced fishermen would just leave him down there and soon he would quit struggling and just swim along with the hook and line. Then when they had several hits they would haul their gear. But we were not willing to do that. At each hit we pulled in the gear to get the precious fish. Since the salmon usually hit the bottom hook first, this meant all the gear had to be removed to get to him. Each line was unhooked and dropped in a five gallon bucket and the hook hung on the side of the bucket. Then the fish was brought in, netted, and put in the ice chest. The hook was re-baited and returned to the down-rigger. Then the remaining gear retrieved from the bucket. If you re-membered the order of the hooks and went in and took them out in reverse order, things worked out pretty well, but if you made a mistake and took the hooks out of sequence the resulting tangle was terrible.

We were awfully proud when we brought our first day's catch in to the buyer at the Tenakee dock. The buyer had a small shed at the end of the dock and she weighed the fish, paid in cash, and iced them for a float-plane pickup the next day. When I displayed our first day's catch in the ice chest, her frown was a disconcerting reminder that although I had a license and some fish, I was still a Chichaco. My next lesson began. The water in the chest was still light pink from the blood of the cleaned fish. So I learned how to really clean the gills and the backbone until there was not one speck of blood left. The blood was what would spoil first, so it was essential that the water the fish were in was absolutely clear. Then there was size. "Hmm," she said, "that one is too small." "Oh well," I said, "I guess we can eat it." "Well," she said, "we are not supposed to do this, but let me show you how to stretch a fish." Over the edge of the bull rail she broke the back bone of the fish in several places. Then she pulled on the head and tail and measured it again. "See," she said, "it is long enough now." And another $37.50 for me.

We were happy and having lots of fun. My partner ran the boat and I worked the gear. But it was also a lot of work, so we invited Hubert, an old friend, up for a couple of weeks of fishing. Hubert liked fishing more than anyone else I knew, and when I explained hand trolling, he was on his way. The day after he arrived by float plane we were on the water, searching for salmon.

We fished for a week or so and each day would take our ice chest full of fish into the buyer at Tenakee. *Raven's* idle speed was a bit too fast for effective King fishing, but we were doing just fine with the Cohos. We might not catch the "big one" but plenty of good, solid Silvers were a fine alternative. Several days we brought in more fish than any of the other fishermen from Tenakee and for that day we were "high liner." We were having a grand time and with all those fish, we really could not complain that the big one got away.

One day, near the end of Hubert's stay, we had fished hard all day without a single strike. I was tired and I wanted to go to the dock and commiserate with Jim Beam on ice. But Hubert was a never-say-die kind of guy. "Let's just give it another little bit," he would say. And I would grumble and give in. Finally I had had enough and I headed *Raven* for home. As we came abreast Corner Bay, Hubert tried once again. "Come on Jofus," he said. (He always called me Jofus when he thought I was acting the fool.) "We've still got a bit of daylight and we've caught a few in the past over there. Let's give Corner Bay one troll through. If they aren't there, we'll bag it." So we headed over and began to rig the gear: set out the weights, lower six feet, hook up a snubber and leader and flasher and more leader and snap in a strip of herring, lower six more feet and do it again, and again. I was really tired and thirsty and not into another futile effort at all.

Well, you can guess the rest of the story. As we turned into Corner Bay the first Silver hit. Before it was in the boat there was another--and another. We were both too busy to keep count. As soon as we got the gear back in the water there was another hit. The ice chest was full. We had no time to clean fish. I found an old canvas sack somewhere and we filled it with fish and put it in the shower and wet it down. Then we just started throwing the Silvers into the skiff up on the boat deck. Splat! Herring scales and salmon blood everywhere. Once, we stopped to catch our breath and looked at each other. There was no gear in the water. We had been too busy landing fish to get the hooks baited and back in. We laughed and laughed and then went back to work.

When dark finally dropped, we headed in. We had caught almost a hundred fish in less than an hour. We didn't catch the big Kings, but the excitement of all those Cohos made up for it. We were high liner that day and with the buyer helping, we cleaned fish well into the night. We divided up the cash, and the next day Hubert flew home.

My partner and I fished a few more days after Hubert left, but it wasn't the same. The fishing seemed routine. I renewed the hand trolling permit for several years, but never fished it again and finally I let it lapse. I continued to buy sport fishing licenses, and from time to time would have a go at it when we were hungry for salmon, but my heart was not in it. Somehow the reality could never quite live up to the memory of hand trolling at Corner Bay and the day it didn't matter whether the big one got away.

16 Genoa Bay Cafe

Aprudent boater tries to avoid the unexpected. Sometimes, however, a surprise can make the day and the trip. When a destination proves delightful beyond expectation, being there can be as much fun as getting there.

As usual, I hauled *Shadow* in the dead of winter, which may be cause to question my prudence. The old story is that if you want to know if you will enjoy boating, put on a plastic raincoat full of holes, get in the shower, turn on the cold water full blast and tear up $50 bills as fast as you can. If you enjoy that, you'll enjoy boating. There is probably nothing, however, that will make a person enjoy a haulout. Even in the best of weather, a boat on the hard is like, well, a fish out of water. A long ladder up and down, drains and toilets that cannot be used, and a bed with a permanent list. But a haulout in winter? If you want to know if you will enjoy that, put on that old plastic raincoat and some leaky gum boots, stomp around in mud for a while, grab some wet sacks of expensive supplies, climb up a twenty-foot, shaky ladder to the shower, turn on the cold water, and try to paint the shower stall while tearing up $100 bills. If you enjoy that, you'll enjoy a winter haulout.

So, pre-empting mutiny by the crew, I offered a dinner out instead of another can of Dennymore stew. We gathered some local knowledge and once more descended the wet ladder, crossed the muddy yard, found the little over-grown golf cart they called an "economy size" rental car and headed off in the general direction we had been given: "down the road that ways a bit."

It was a dark and foggy night. And, of course, the car had neither GPS nor radar. We followed the pavement to its end, flipped a coin, and parked beside the dimly lit sign: Genoa Bay Café.

We were a bit early, but still surprised and somewhat cautious that the dining room was entirely empty. It was like entering a new anchorage that looks appealing but no other boats are there. Is something wrong? Have I overlooked something? Not only were there no diners, there was no host, no cook, no anybody.

After a couple of "hello's," Ben appeared, and because he was dressed in white I assumed he was a cook. Protracted negotiations about whether or not the café was in fact open and whether or not a private party was expected were inconclusive, but eventually we found a booth in the general direction Ben had waved.

Then nothing happened. Ben disappeared. After what seemed an appropriate waiting time, I wandered back toward the kitchen in search of food and drink. Again Ben appeared. In response to my question, he waved at the wine rack: "Yea, we have wine, help yourself." I picked a Georges Duboeuf Beaujolais and Ben handed me a couple of glasses. "Want me to open that for you?" He asked. I allowed that I had my Swiss Army Knife and could manage just fine on my own. Ben went back to wherever he had come from.

About half way through the bottle, Ben showed up at our table. "Sorry you've had to wait," he said, "John seems to be a little late. I thought this might tide you over. "Complements of the house."

Ben placed before us one of the most beautiful plates of ante-pasta I have ever seen. We began to realize that the meal might develop in unexpectedly interesting ways. Actually, to call the plate ante-pasta is to do it less than justice. There was Ciabatta bread, drenched in outstanding balsamic vinegar and olive oil and topped with amazingly tasty pesto. Olives, bits of cheeses, peppers, beautiful sun-dried tomatoes, and several other visual and edible delights. With the last half of the wine, things were picking up.

By the time we had finished the ante-pasta and the wine, John had arrived and dinner seemed in the offing. At least we got a menu. We took our menus to the kitchen counter for a general discussion. After considerable debate, Ben, now aided by Fernando and John, admitted that they did have one order of prime rib left over. It didn't take much effort, however, to elicit the information that all three recommended a steak instead. Which cut? But this time I just let them decide for themselves. It seemed that was the direction things were headed anyway, and it's always easier to ride the horse the direction he's going. The crew ordered vegetable lasagna.

Fortified by another bottle of wine, a Canadian wine recommended by John that proved to be excellent, a bit heavier than the Bordeaux and exactly right for the main course, we returned to our table.

The presentation of the main course left us almost speechless. The two large plates were gorgeous. The vegetable lasagna was topped with heaping sautéed onions and surrounded with various tidbits and morsels of salad makings. My tenderloin was smothered in a caper sauce and accompanied by a plate heaping with beautifully presented and separately prepared vegetables--cold pickled beets, small red potatoes, peppers, onions, squashes.

Although neither of us are big eaters and the portions were gargantuan, we both ate every bite. That one meal was worth the trip.

Continuing our prudent boating practices, we waited until after returning home to check the cruising guides and the internet. Genoa Bay Café, a part of the Genoa Bay Marina, is owned by Ben and Will Kiedaisch. (The ubiquitous Ben?) The website is as thoughtful and delightful as the restaurant. First stop on our next trip north will be Genoa Bay Marina and Café. I think I'll try the rack of lamb...

How to get there without including the haulout and rental car? Clear customs in Sidney or Tsehum Harbour, head north to Satellite Channel, turn east into Cowichan Bay and turn right into Genoa Bay. From there, you are on your own. After all, isn't the unexpected part of the adventure?

17 The Best Of South East Alaska: Ketchikan To Baranof Warm Springs

Ketchikan to Meyers Chuck--35 miles
Meyers Chuck to Anan Creek--50 miles
Anan Creek to Wrangell--15 miles
Wrangell to Portage Bay--63 miles
Portage Bay to Baranof Warm Springs--55 miles

It's a short run from Ketchikan to Meyers Chuck, but the transition is huge. After the cruise-ship madness of Alaska's First City, Meyers Chuck is a return to sanity. Kings and Silvers cluster outside the harbor, so if I arrive near slack I go looking for dinner. The entry to the harbor is narrow, but deep enough. Just keep the charted rock to starboard and stay between the lines. Red right returning! There is a small dock and room for about three boats to swing, so a back-up is Vixon Harbor or Union Bay.

Next stop: Anan Creek. It's the best place to watch bears fish for salmon. The anchorage isn't much because the shallow bay shoals quickly. But it is possible to get a hook down well enough to go ashore. The Forest Service maintains a viewing platform near the falls, and a wooden walkway from the shore. Some of the

Sitka

Baranof
Warm Springs

Portage Bay

Petersburg ■

Wrangell ■

Anan Creek

Meyers Chuck

Ketchikan ■

Scale in Miles

0   10 20 30 40 50   100

N

bears are adept fishermen, watching carefully and then a quick snap of the teeth and a meal. Others are somewhere lower on the learning curve, falling in the water, missing their lunge, trying again. There is also a pecking order, lower status acquiescing to those further up the chain. All bears are not created equal.

Permits are required now and difficult to get because commercial guides buy them up quickly. Regulations change frequently so you need to contact the Forest Service well ahead of time.

After Anan Creek the next stop is Wrangell. It is a piece of small town Americana to be in Wrangell for the Fourth of July. Wrangell is too small for the cruise liners, so, while it doesn't elicit visions of gold, glamour and grandeur like Ketchikan or Skagway, it also has not been destroyed by tourists. Chief attraction on the Fourth is the internationally famous Wrangell Alaska Boom Box Marching Band. Unable to field enough musicians or their instruments, the enterprising citizens of Wrangell assemble forty or fifty marchers with their portable tape payers. On signal from the drum major they all press the start buttons simultaneously, or almost simultaneously, and head down Main Street in perfect formation and step. It is a sight to bring tears to your eyes and laughter to your heart.

Until it was recently enlarged, the Wrangell harbor was tiny and guest moorage not really a priority. On one visit, the harbor master directed me to dock space along the main float. For *Sundown* this required a 180 in a narrow channel and edging to barely sufficient dock space between rafted purse seiners. *Sundown*, sixty-four feet and eighty-one tons, was a single screw and did not carry thrusters. Of course, if I were around yachts, there would have been a slew of people out there wanting to take lines, fend off, and generally help us fit in. The sein crews, however, following the traditions of their trade, waited to be asked. They were also enjoying the anticipation of watching me make a fool of myself. Fortunately that day, tide, wind and *Sundown's* 52x38 prop cooperated, and with much backing and filling we finally and somewhat gracefully sidled up to the dock. Now the fishermen, deprived of a show, quickly and efficiently helped us secure our lines.

When I first became a "boater," whatever that is, I watched the yachts come and go and thought the way to dock a boat was to send the crew to the foredeck and yell a lot. It seemed to be a dangerous undertaking, requiring people on the boat and ashore, throwing lines and generally behaving as if docking a boat was a mysterious skill, requiring as many people as were available and yelled instructions from everyone. Then I began to watch the fishermen: one boat, one man. I watched as they quietly brought their boat to rest at the dock, stepped off, and secured their lines. There was something to learn here. Next day I snuck off to a deserted dock away from helping hands and laughing eyes and practiced. Over and over I brought her in to port and in to starboard. I worked with her lines so I could dock her, step off with the lines and tie her up. I practiced until I had it.

You can learn a lot watching fishermen if you can find any left to watch. There used to be nearly a hundred commercial boats in Friday Harbor. Now there is one. I was fortunate, however, to have many teachers around. When "boaters" finally make it to the dock with their crew, bow thrusters, stern thrusters, twin screws, and help from other boaters fore and aft, they most frequently throw lines to the dock and expect the dock handlers to adjust the lengths. For the fishermen, if there is someone on the dock to take a line, it is tied to the dock and the boat crew is left to make the final adjustments. Sensible!

There are two steps to securing a boat at the dock and failure to distinguish these two different operations causes a great deal of needless trouble. Step one is to get the boat and the dock tied to each other. This can be done in any fashion that accomplishes the purpose. Step two then requires adjusting the lines, adding springs as necessary, and, in the best of all worlds, flemishing the lines.

From Wrangell, it's through Wrangell Narrows, with its seventy-six navigation aids and six ranges, not to be attempted in the dark or fog. At the northern end of the Narrows lies Petersburg, a decent Scandinavian village with several good shops and the largest fish processing plant remaining in Southeast. Time to re-provision. I like to call Hammer and Wikan Grocery, for a free shuttle to and from the store.

From Petersburg, a turn to port thrusts us into Frederick Sound and the first sightings of bergy bits and growlers, small chunks of glacier ice floating down from the Le Conte Glacier and the Stikene Ice Field. I scoop up a small chunk and get ready for the best martini west of Oscar's at the Waldorf. The ice has been compressed for ten thousand years and all the air squeezed out. What is left is pure glacier water, frozen like a rock, clear as a diamond. A chunk will last for days in the ice chest, or even just left on the deck. The martinis are clear, cold, and delicious, given that the quality of the gin is worthy of the ice.

Portage Bay offers a good overnight, clear approach and plenty of swinging room. Frederick Sound is a playground for whales and porpoises. It's not unusual to see Dall's, orcas, humpbacks and Grays between Portage Bay and Point Gardner.

After Frederick Sound, I head for my favorite of all the mysterious and magical places in Southeast: Baranof Warm Springs. After the long trip north I drop hook here and just hang out for a couple of weeks.

When I came the first time, the old store, once supported on pilings above the tide line, was precariously cantilevered from shore. The young couple who ran the store, two of legions of dreamers and visionaries who have sought their freedom and fortune on the frontier, were a joy to meet. Their young daughter augmented the family income by selling moon snail egg cases, carefully and gently nestled in cotton in match boxes. At low tide, moon snails themselves were sometimes about and a quick grab and twist out of the shell provided a delicacy equal to abalone, with a beautiful shell and operculum for memories. Old bath cubicles lined the trail ashore, like a miniature tourist court from the 30's. Each cubicle contained an old claw footed tub, porcelain pealing and plumbing rusting, filled with the wonderful healing water piped from the springs. The water ran continuously, and the tubs were kept full by a length of plastic pipe in the drain, maintaining a chin high water level. There was a small bench or a broken chair and a couple of coat hooks on the wall; scraps of linoleum on the floor. A soak was fifty cents.

Sanitary? Probably not. Healing? Definitely; of both body and spirit.

Then as now, cold water for refilling your tanks is piped from the river to an old hose on the dock. Sanitary? Probably not. Pure? Absolutely!

Baranof is hardly a village; perhaps a community. Twelve houses perch along the tide line, connected by a stout boardwalk. The old store has fallen into the salt chuck, and is replaced by a more modern and modest structure, safely ashore, and sometimes open. Garbage and sewage, no longer thrown to the cleansing tide, must be carted. The tubs and their little cubicles are gone, but recently replaced by more modern and appealing small rooms with enticing tubs. The tidal grid remains, used, if at all, only in the direst of emergencies. At the end of the boardwalk a mighty waterfall plunges from above. In the old days a Pelton wheel, powered by this immense hydro power, provided electricity for the community. Homes were radiantly heated by hot water from the springs. The annual utility bill for the entire community was $7.00 for grease for the Pelton wheel. Now the wheel is rusting quietly beside its flue, and electricity is provided by individual generators for the various houses. So much for community, so much for progress, so much for free electricity and quiet.

Nevertheless, in spite of generators and the loss of the old store, Baranof remains my favorite place in all Southeast. From the boardwalk you can take a trail up the mountain past six pools of hot spring water. Take the spur to the left, climb a primitive and muddy trail and you reach the world's most glorious hot springs pool. Actually there are three pools, but the first two are too hot for me. The third, a natural grotto in the hard granite, improved gently over time by unnamed benefactors, is waist deep with several convenient sitting rocks; temperature 101 degrees Fahrenheit. It is so close to the head of the great waterfall, that cold spray bathes your face as you soak in the healing mineral water. Protocol requires one to soap up and wash off outside the pool before entering. And while occasionally you find Bud Lite cans or a dirty towel, for the most part the pool remains pristine and inviting. Clothing is optional.

Fred Bahovec, who lived at Baranof until his death several years ago at 102, attributed his health and longevity to the healing properties of Baranof Warm Springs. Fred was on to something and he told of his life at Baranof in The First 100 Years. The day after his one hundredth birthday party, Fred began writing his second book, The Next 100 Years.

After your soak, you can continue up the rough main trail to beautiful Baranof Lake where in the old days a canoe lay ashore, ready for whomever wished a tranquil paddle.

Between the picture-perfect lake and the head of the falls, a short, swift river is filled with cutthroat. If you are tired of fare from the sea, salmon, halibut, crab, prawns, ling cod, and so on, enjoy fresh trout for dinner. At first my trout catching was sparse. Then one year as I plied the river again and again, I heard a voice behind me: "What are you doing, boy?" I turned to see a small black woman with a halo of curly white hair. "Well," I said, "I'm fishing for some dinner." "How are you doing?" "Not too bad." "Let me see." Thus forced, I showed her my one meager cutthroat. "Humpf," she said, "got a knife?" She deftly cut a small filet from my dinner and hooked it to my spinner. "Now," she said, "throw it right over there. You are reeling too slow. Reel a bit faster." Soon I had four good, solid Cuts for dinner.

Thus was my introduction to Clothilde Bahovec, Fred's widow, who continued to live at Baranof for years beyond his death until she joined him. Heaven for Fred and Clothilde cannot be much different from Baranof.

Clothilde answered to "Mermaid" on the VHF, and each year as Sundown entered the bay, my call brought her to the dock to help with the lines and to share stories and gossip and dinner.

Clothilde taught me where to dig for the best clams, and led me through the narrow pass into the salt lagoon where she showed me Joe's old boat, sunk to the bottom, and also how to pick fresh goose tongue for our salad. She showed me where the halibut holes were and where it was easiest to catch Coho or Kings. We picked low bush blueberries and high bush huckleberries together, always on the watch for grizzlies, who considered the huckleberries to be their own private preserve. And she shared warmth, humor, and wisdom that are rare on this earth.

After that, each year I would anchor in the same spot, around the corner from the waterfall and dock. I would sit there at anchor for two weeks. Each day I would skiff to the dock, walk up the trail for a soak, and then on to the lake. Later, there was visiting at the store or on the dock. Trash was taken ashore at low tide and burned at the tide line. The ashes were always cleaned away by the power of the tide. Occasionally another boat would anchor in our bay, but they would leave after a night or two. And sometimes sport fishermen would come through in a skiff, hoping to see our eagles or bear or even catch our fish.

At the head of our little anchorage, a small stream emptied into the bay. Each evening, after the fishermen left, a grizzly sow would bring her two cubs down to the outlet of the stream to fish. The twins stayed with her for three years and we were thrilled to watch them morph from clumsy little teddy bears who could care less about salmon to skilled young salmon hunters.

There were plenty of fish: pollock, rock cod, and ling cod to be had in exchange for a few herring. Twice I fed not only ourselves but most of the community with seventy-five pound halibuts.

One year my friend Al Vreeland was aboard, celebrating his seventieth birthday. All week he had desperately wanted to catch a halibut, and all week we had been skunked. I tried every halibut hole and trick I knew, but none was to be had. On his last evening, Al's disappointment was palpable. Just before bedtime, I told him to bait up and leave his offering in the water overnight. He complied, but without much enthusiasm. After all, we had worked at it all week. What would this non-work produce?

I was usually first up, and after I had my coffee, I checked the aft deck. Sure enough, something big was on the deep end of Al's line. On deck in his pajamas, he began the long process of moving a barn door to the surface. A hooked large halibut will sometimes lie flat on the mud bottom and the suction defies detaching him. Sometimes you can strum on the line and slight irritation will cause the giant to loosen, or perhaps thump your rod on the boat railing. Another tactic to break the suction is to go off some distance so the angle of pull is reduced and attempt to slide the fish along the bottom until he decides to cooperate.

Fortunately this morning the halibut was a bit more cooperative and eventually he emerged from the depths. He lay there on the surface, wondering what was next. We also wondered. It was about six feet from the waterline to the deck. We had a gaff, but a gaffed halibut can be an explosive critter, both on the way to the boat and after reaching the deck. Standard procedure at this point was to shoot the halibut just behind the eyes, producing a stun that would permit boarding. So the 22 rifle came from below decks and I administered the lethal shot. In this case, however, the shot produced exactly the opposite of the expected quiescence. Al's halibut took off across the surface of the bay as if he were jet propelled. Water flew as his tail beat the surface. Al's reel screamed until the line ran out. We watched as Al's halibut disappeared around the point trailing two hundred yards of line. Al flew home without his halibut, but with laughter in his heart and an indelible memory of the halibut that would not be caught.

The next time I was in town I bought a harpoon designed specifically to deal with these situations. Rather than being shot, the halibut is harpooned and secured with a substantial line. Besides, it is now so difficult to bring a gun across Canadian borders that it isn't worth the trouble. But there is more here; now I know better. Those large halibut are almost always female brood stock and should be left to go about their business. Besides, a ten or fifteen pound "chicken" halibut is just fine, and much easier to clean.

One evening as several of us sat around a campfire near the store, Mr. Lee motored slowly into the bay. All the locals there knew Mr. Lee. He had come from Tokyo last year in his 32 foot sloop in search of halibut. Although he fished all summer, the halibut eluded him. Here he came again this year, towing something behind his boat, a one-hundred pound halibut. I don't know how cross-cultural congratulations really work, but Mr. Lee was definitely the hero of the day in Baranof. Although he was beside himself with delight and pride, it was clear he had not a clue what to do with his trophy. With some tact, several of us helped him get the fish on to the dock, and then with a rope through the gills we dragged it up to the fire. Knowledgeable hands made quick work of filleting, and we all enjoyed roasting a chunk on the fire. The rest was divided up, as was the custom. I don't know what happened to the ears. It was a good end to another good day at Baranof.

18 Finally: Baranof Warm Springs To Glacier Bay

Baranof Warm Springs to Sitka--84 miles
Sitka to Kimshan Cove --57 miles
Kimshan Cove to Elfin Cove--61 miles
Elfin Cove to Bartlett Cove--30 miles
Bartlett Cove to Reid Inlet--33 miles

Sitka is the oldest and most interesting city in Southeast Alaska. The traditional homeland of the Tlingit people, headquarters for the Russian fur traders and soldiers, the site of the official transfer of Seward's Folly from the Russians to the Americans, and Alaska's first capital, Sitka embodies much of the history and mystique of Alaska. James Michener lived here and worked at Sheldon Jackson College while writing his monumental Alaska; there are two magnificent museums, old growth forests, ravens, eagles, whales, salmon, and, of course, cruise ships.

Sitka is the ancestral home of the Kiksadi Clan of the Tlingit people, and for them, "Sitka" meant "by the sea." According to an ancient Tlingit legend, Raven created the world and established the Tlingit people in this region at the beginning of time.

According to European anthropologists, The Tlingit people are descendants of the interior Athabaskan people, who in turn are descendants of the Chukchi people of eastern Siberia. Chukchi people crossed the Bering Land Bridge from Siberia to Alaska 30,000 years ago, about the same time that the Paleolithic people of Europe were establishing themselves in the Pyrenees and later producing the great cave art at Lascaux, Trois-Freres, and Niaux.

In 1740 the Danish explorer, Vitus Bering, was the first European to visit Alaska. Employed by Peter the Great, and following a plan devised by the Russian Emperor, he built two small vessels, *St. Peter* and the *St. Paul*, on the Kamchatka Peninsula and sailed them to the Aleutian Islands. Bering's story, beginning with a 6000 mile marathon trek across Siberia to the Kamchatka Peninsula, is both heroic and tragic and Michener's telling of it is well worth reading. Russian fur traders followed Bering, and in 1799 Alexander Baranof built a fort a few miles north of present-day Sitka. The Tlingits who lived there had an elaborate culture and established way of life thousands of years old. They objected to the Russian invasion and in 1802 led by a fierce warrior, Kot-le-an, they attacked the fort and massacred most of the Russians and a number of Alutes the Russians had enslaved to work as retrievers for the otters they killed. Two years later the Russians counter attacked and after a fierce battle drove the Tlingits into the forest. In the unfortunate blending of bloody profiteering and self righteous religion, the Russians renamed the site "New Archangel."

In the 1867 the Americans bought Alaska from the Russians for $7,200,000--about $12 per square mile. Now the Tlingits who had been forced by the Russians to learn the Russian language, were forced to abandon Russian and learn English. Presbyterian missionaries replaced Orthodox Christianity imposed by priests and profiteers with Presbyterian Christianity enforced by missionaries and soldiers. When the Tlingit objected, the US Navy shelled the villages of Kake and Wrangell in 1869 and destroyed Angoon in 1882, solidifying US control. Thus, the Russians and Americans attempted to civilize the ancient Tlingit culture in the 18th and 19th centuries just as the Russians and the Americans have attempted to civilize the people of Afghanistan, Iraq, and Iran, home of the oldest cultures in the western world, in the 20th and 21st centuries.

Smallpox, introduced by Europeans in 1835-1839, decimated the Tlingit more effectively than muskets and bibles and left the field open for Catholics, Anglicans, United Church, Protestants, Mormons and Pentecostals to convert the few surviving Tlingit to "modern" religion. The bawdy and raucous shamanic myths of Raven and his cronies, Wolf, Eagle, and Killer Whale, were replaced by stories of Adam, Noah, Sodom and Gomorrah.

The Tlingit culture is experiencing resurgence today as artists, carvers, and story tellers work in Sitka. A beautiful Tlingit Mystical Warrior carved and painted by Peter Charile of the Capilano Reservation far to the south hangs above my computer.

Sitka is also home to Mike and Mim McConnell who for many years lived aboard their boat, *Gwynfyd*, before they swallowed the hook and moved ashore. I first met Mike and Mim at Baranof Warm Springs and our friendship flourished each summer for several years. Mike is working on a sequel to his first book, Hand Troller. Mim is a graphic artist, web designer, photographer, and all-around Renaissance woman. She is the Mayor of Sitka.

Even before fishing, logging, oil drilling and tourism exploited the riches of Alaska, the fur traders had their way with the virgin country. The fur trade was fabulously lucrative for the Russians, who traded the luxuriant sea otter pelts to wealthy Europeans and Chinese. First the Russians and then the Americans used torture and murder to enslave the gentle Alutes and even the less gentle Tlingits, forcing these people who had survived for centuries in these islands and waters to participate in the carnage. The friendly, curious, and inquisitive sea otters were unafraid and their slaughter by Russian muskets was ruthless, bloody, and deadly, both for otters and people. The muskets fired until their barrels were red hot. Aleut and Tlingit slaves were sent into the frigid water like bird dogs to retrieve the dead otters although ninety percent of the bodies had already sunk beyond reach. If the native slaves refused, they, too, were shot or tortured, merely collateral damage to the slaughter of the sea otters. Even the ten percent recovery rate was sufficient to maintain a lucrative fur trade until the 1850's when the otters had almost all been killed.

When the otters were gone, the Russians and Americans left. As with subsequent exploitation for gold, timber, fish and oil, the exploiting industries ravished their resource until they forced themselves out of business.

As always, the massacre was legitimated and the murders exonerated by religion. St. Michael's Cathedral, the oldest Orthodox Cathedral in the Western Hemisphere, was built in Sitka in 1844.

Today Sitka is a joy to visit. The Pioneer's home provides state supported retirement facilities for all Alaska residents. Tlingit artists are at work in shops and museums. St. Michael's Cathedral and the ancient Bishops House display some of the most precious icons to be found in the Western Hemisphere. The islands that protect Sitka from the full force of Pacific storms are pristine. Mt. Edgecumbe, when not shrouded in clouds, is magnificent. Bears, eagles, ravens, and salmon find homes nearby.

From Sitka the route north winds through Olga Strait and Neva Strait to Salisbury Sound. The FVF (Fast Vehicle Ferry) *Fairweather* runs between Sitka and Juneau and it's a good idea to listen carefully to the VHF to avoid meeting the ferry in the straits. I try to leave Sitka in time to be in Salisbury about an hour before slack tide because this is where we fish for salmon. There are several hot spots: off Kalinin Bay, Sinitsin Island, Point Kruzof, and between Morskoi Rock and Sea Rock. I usually follow the local fishing boats. At least one advantage of the cruise business is that local charter boats fish the area, and they know where the salmon are. With dinner on board, there may be time to visit the colony of sea otters at the Klokachef Islands before heading for one of the several delightful anchorages in Salisbury Sound or inside Kakul Narrows.

Before I moved to the Pacific Northwest and fell in love with the Inside Passage, I fished the high mountain lakes and streams of Colorado and Montana for the magnificent brook, cutthroat, and rainbow trout. There is something pure, pristine, and simple about fly fishing for trout. An ancient split bamboo rod, eventually retired in favor of Orvis graphite, a single action reel, double tapered line, some leader, and a small collection of Royal Coachmen, Humpies, Mosquitoes and Black Gnats was enough. Hip boots, an old wicker creel with damp willow leaves in the bottom, and a small landing net completed the gear list. The pace was slow, intense, and relaxed. On hookup, the action was simple. A wild trout on one end of the line and my left hand on the other end: a gentle and subtle tug of war with the winner determined by wit, skill, and luck.

Then I moved to the Northwest and the scenario changed. Fishing for salmon is definitely gear-intensive. You need a boat, depth sounder, heavy salmon rods, substantial Penn reels with adjustable drag, downriggers, ten pound leads, release mechanisms, a hardware store full of spoons, hoochies, herring strips, plugs, flashers, swivels, a huge unwieldy landing net, and hundreds of yards of monofilament.

And then, after you learn to manipulate all this gear, you have to learn where the salmon are. As with real estate, salmon fishing is about location, location, location. First in *Elsa* and then in *Raven* I dragged weights, spoons, flashers, hoochies, herring strips and herring plugs through the deep and mysterious waters of the San Juan Islands for countless days before I began to figure it out. Finally I located my special fishing holes: the two submerged pinnacles off Carter Point, Boulder Reef, Point Lawrence, and the navigation marker at Post Point. I learned that it is not a matter of being in the vicinity; you have to be dead on--thirty feet one way or the other does not work.

Gear intensive, rainy weather, and illusive salmon can be frustrating. But all is forgotten at the call of "fish on." With that signal, as the line screams off the reel, a definite protocol sets in. All hands join the drill and the focus is absolute and electric. The helmsman brings the engines to neutral, marks the exact location of the strike, either by triangulation or GPS, and then devotes total attention to keeping the boat off the rocks.

On the back deck all hands attend the dancing rod. The hook is set, the drag checked, and the rod handed to the designated fisherman. Gratuitous advice arrives from all quarters: "Keep the rod tip up." "Let him run." "Watch out, he's turning, reel faster." "Don't touch the drag." And while instructions are barked and advice liberally voiced, all hands turn to clearing the decks for battle. The other fishing lines are retrieved and the rods stowed on the side decks, the downriggers cranked up, and the weights secured. The focus of the entire crew is intense. Eventually the quarry reveals himself: if a King he heads for the depths, if a Coho he clears the surface in a sparkling spray as he attempts to throw the hook. Eventually he tires and is led to the side of the boat. The magnificent salmon glows iridescent green and silver beneath the surface. Now comes the moment of truth. More fish are lost when they are spooked by the landing net than at any other time. The net must be surreptitiously lowered into the water and carefully brought up under the fish. The temptation to scoop at him is great, but the results disastrous. One hint of the net and he is off again. Netted and gasping on the deck, he is admired by all. Pictures are taken. A blow by a ceremonial club ends his struggle and the rich, orange fish is cleaned and washed until every bit of blood is removed, and he is slipped into the cooler filled with salt water. The fish keeps much better in 58 degree salt water than in ice where the fresh water begins immediately to break down the flesh.

In the past I would sometimes return to fishing, but now I generally quit when there is enough to eat. I like to believe that my practice falls close to the ethic of traditional people: catch what you can eat, honor the animal that feeds you, and, with thanks, enjoy the meal. Although with fish getting even more scarce and regulations even more stringent, I'm finding it's hardly worth the effort anymore. So sad!

But if we do fish and if we are lucky, with dinner aboard and the fishing gear stowed, we head for Kakul Narrows and anchorage for the night. There are several good anchorages in the area, so just take your pick. That evening, alder chips on the grill add their distinctive smoky flavor to the grilled salmon, replicating an ancient and traditional method of cooking.

The trip through Peril Strait is quintessential Alaska. There is a considerable tidal current and a narrow channel marked by seventeen navigational aids, so sailing with the tide is a good idea. Peril Strait is not named for this intricate passage, but rather for a famous banquet thrown by local Tlingit people for early European fur traders. The main course was clam chowder poisoned by deadly algae from a red tide algae bloom. The fatal results did not contribute to peaceful cross cultural understanding.

Peril Strait empties into Hoonah Sound, a great place to watch for orcas and humpbacks. Morris Reef, at the confluence of Chatham Sound is good halibut fishing.

From Florence Bay it is two hours south to Baranof Warm Springs. Anchored at Baranof, we visit the hot springs, fish for trout in the river, watch the grizzlies, and mellow out. Day trips explore Tenakee Springs, Basket Bay, Kelp Bay, Cosmos Cove, Kasnyku Bay, Waterfall Cove, Takatz Bay, and, most especially, Red Bluff Bay. Gray, humpback and orca whales frequent Point Gardner.

A float plane comes to take us home. From the dock at Baranof a twenty minute flight over Baranof Lake and the Mount Bassie ice field delivers us in Sitka. Two hours more by jet, and we are back in Seattle.

From Sitka to Baranof provides a week full of adventure, but if time permits us two weeks, we visit Glacier Bay. From Sitka, we head north through Salisbury Sound and out into the open ocean until we tuck back inside at Ogden passage and a quiet anchorage in the eerily beautiful Kimshan Cove. Then a dip in one of the best hot springs in the Northwest: White Sulphur Springs. It's a bit of a trick getting there, but worth every bit of it. Don Douglass and

Reanne Hemingway-Douglass tell you exactly how to do it in Exploring Southeast Alaska.

The best route to Glacier Bay is through Lisianski Strait with perhaps a side trip to the Native village of Pellican where provisions and repairs are available. The next stop is Elfin Cove, a unique Scandinavian village perched on boardwalks around a small harbor. There is a tiny store, friendly people, and lots of atmosphere. If Dave Walton is there, he is the best guy in the entire Northwest for electronic gear purchase or repair. If the harbor is full, I head for Inian Cove which I share with a colony of sea otters.

Glacier Bay, when visited by George Vancouver in 1794, was filled with ice to the entrance at Icy Strait. John Muir visited in 1879 and was largely responsible for Glacier Bay eventually becoming a national monument and park. Archeological and anthropological evidence suggests that the ice was not so advanced earlier and that it was the home of Tlingit people who inhabited the lower bay for many centuries until about three hundred years ago when the glaciers advanced. Since then, the glaciers have again been in retreat. Now, with global warming well underway, the glaciers are retreating at an alarming rate. The Glacier Bay website provides graphic evidence of the glacier retreat.

Visitor pressure on Glacier Bay is immense and the Park Service does its best to balance environmental preservation with tourist access. The number of cruise liners is restricted as is the number of pleasure boats, and advance reservations are required. Inside the park there is a whole world: a sea lion rookery which you can smell from a mile away, whales, bears, sea otters, moose, and rare and magnificent tufted puffins. Anchorages are deep and isolated, but there are many. My favorites are at the head of Reid

Glacier and in North Sandy Cove where a moose frequently stops by in the late afternoon.

Glacier Bay provides a journey back in time. Hundreds of feet above the waterline the basalt cliffs are scared by striations left by the ever moving glaciers. At the head of each inlet there is no vegetation, just as it was at the end of the last ice age, but as you retreat from the head of inlet, moving toward the more open water, first lichen and then algae emerge; then come the mosses and ferns, then scrub willow and alder. Finally, all the flora and fauna of the rain forest greet us and we feel that we have made a journey of ten thousand years in two hours.

Leaving Glacier Bay, the bow points south into Icy Strait. We have traversed the Inside Passage, learned its lessons in natural history, environmental destruction and protection, anthropology, cross cultural communication and exploitation, maritime custom and skills, navigation, salmon, eagles, and wilderness. And perhaps we have learned something about ourselves, our assumptions, and our perspectives.

19 RETURN TO GWA'YI

No one knows how long people have lived at Gwa'yi. Village
Elders tell an ancient story that the people of the village are
descendants of two wolves, Kwalili and Kawadilikala, who were
the fathers of the Dzawada'enuxw and Haxwa'mis people who
founded the villages of Alalxu and Gwa'yi and who gave birth to
the first human beings at the beginning of time. Anthropologists
have found archeological evidence nearby of human occupancy
for ten thousand years. Located on Kingcome River, three kilometers from the head of Kingcome Inlet, Gwa'yi is unique on
the Northwest coast because it is the only village site that has
been continually occupied since remote times. European settlers
moved every other village in the Northwest from its original site,
either because they wanted it for themselves or to contribute to
cultural destruction. Only Gwa'yi was never moved, perhaps because of its remote and difficult location.

The people who live at Gwa'yi have been shaped for untold
generations by art, history, ceremony, and survival. A group of
the Kwakwaka'wakw culture, the people of Gwa'yi have been a
source of magnificent ceremonial art and tradition, celebrating

a rich, thriving, and sustainable culture for hundreds of years. Individuals trace their lineage to parents, grandparents, and great-grandparents for dozens of generations. Today Gwa'yi proudly retains not only its illustrious past, but a renewed, vibrant present, as well as a brilliant vision of the future. Old buildings, art, and magic are there, as well as new buildings, new art, and new energy. As with all great cultures, the art and ceremony at Gwa'yi preserve the past and envision the future. The culture celebrates life that is rooted in a particular place and a particular history, but one that also reaches out to engage a much larger world.

I learned of Gwa'yi after coming to the Pacific Northwest thirty-three years ago. From Seattle I flew Harbor Air to Bellingham, where I was to interview for a job as dean of a college. On that fine clear day the four-seat Cessna flew at a thousand feet over territory I had never seen nor even imagined. The San Juan Islands were deep green shapes in a royal blue sea. The Olympic Mountains to the west and the Cascade Mountains to the east were blistering white with fresh snow. I had heard of the San Juan Islands but until that ride in the Cessna, I could not imagine why anyone would want to live there. Now, I can't imagine why anyone would want to live anywhere else. I sometimes think that people who have grown up in the Northwest don't fully realize the magical beauty surrounding them. We landed in Bellingham where the airport was then a one room cinderblock building and a chain-link fence.

Four days of academic interviews were relieved by excursions into the outside world. We hiked from Chuckanut Drive up a short steep trail to Fragrance Lake, toured Whatcom Falls and Arroyo Park. We visited the Lummi Indian Reservation and had lunch in the Fairhaven historic district. On that first trip I knew that there was magic going on in this great Northwest; and I knew this was a place I wanted to live. I couldn't quite place it, or give name to it, but I knew I was into something.

I got the job and moved with my family to Bellingham. The next few years were years of exploration and discovery. At first, it was about being out of doors - skiing, hiking, fishing - the wilderness; it was also about places: Seattle, Victoria, Vancouver, the Olympic Peninsula, Sol Duc Hot Springs, Olympic Hot Springs, Neah Bay, Port Townsend, Mt. Baker, Coleman Glacier, Roosevelt Glacier, Marblemount, Gold Bar, Monte Cristo. Then I began to sense a deeper feeling of finally being home. Thirty years later, my children have moved on, and I have moved on from the university, but the Northwest is still home for me. Over time I came to understand that this tangle of islands, the native cultures, water, mountains, fishing, skiing, and boats carried me into places inside myself that I had not known existed. As the song says, I was coming home to a place I had never been before. As I write now, a third of a century later, I still wonder about my love and connection to this place. My mind returns again to these places, to these times and experiences. I have always been here, and, it is all brand new.

Soon after moving to the Pacific Northwest I read Margaret Craven's book, I Heard the Owl Call My Name. The book was on the New York Times Best Seller List and was made into a movie and a TV mini-series. It is a story about Gwa'yi, and the struggle of the people who live there to survive in the face of encroaching European settlers. Plagued by government efforts to destroy their way of life and by poverty created as settlers appropriated the natural resources that had supported their life and culture for countless generations, they are caught in a dilemma. They can abandon their village and way of life, move into the world of white people and lose their culture, or they can stay in Gwa'yi and die.

The central character in the book is not a native of the village but a young Anglican priest who is sent there by his wise bishop. It is a story about return and reversal. The one who comes as the giver is in fact the receiver. The priest is saved from himself by the truth, beauty, and integrity of the people who have lived close to the land and water for thousands of years.

When I closed the book I opened a world. I didn't know where Gwa'yi was or how to get there but I knew I had to go. I'm not sure why I felt such compulsion. I knew the village was on Kingcome Inlet, somewhere north of Vancouver and that it would be a long boat trip. I needed a boat. Never mind that I had not a clue how to find Kingcome Inlet or how to operate a boat. I was on a mission and set off to Squalicum Harbor where at that time the fishing boats out-numbered the pleasure boats.

We walked the docks. I liked the sleek power boats that looked like jet airplanes frozen in motion. My wife, however, knew more than I did. She had sailed the Inland Waterway from Woods Hole to Jamaica. So, my nautical education began. "That's a Herreshoff," she would say. "But I want a boat with a motor." I would say. "Walt says," she would say, "in boats, function follows form. If it isn't pretty, it will not perform." "We cannot afford pretty," I would say. "We need charts," she would say. "What are charts?" I would ask.

Quan Yin, who protects all sailors, took pity. There, tied to the main dock was *Elsa*. She had a motor, she was attractive, and the price was affordable. Her owner, Ward Williams, was aboard. Ward was a retired Federal Appeals Judge from Seattle and *Elsa* was his love and joy. He had built her from plans provided by George Calkins and he had built to tolerances of no greater than 1/16 of an inch. Ward had named *Elsa* after his mother so maybe that tells you something. We talked with Ward for a while and then bought his boat.

Over time I got to know Ward a bit. My politics are somewhere out in left field. Ward played on the other team with Attila the Hun. But, as we all know, around boats, politics are irrelevant. So we became good sparring partners. I asked Ward how he made his judicial decisions. His reply was neither left nor right, but classic. "Well," he said, "I read all the documents, the arguments, the briefs, the affidavits, the declarations, and I consider all the legal precedents. And then sometimes, I just lean back in my chair, close my eyes, and apply the 'taint fair' principle - it just taint fair." Ward was my kind of judge and my kind of boater.

In addition to being a member of the Grand Old Party, Ward was also something of a Spartan, and this showed in *Elsa*. There was a windshield wiper, but instead of an electric motor there was a little bronze handle. Working the handle worked the wiper. Simple. As a matter of fact, as I have advanced (if it is an advance) through various other boats with their many eccentric electric wipers, more than once I have wished for *Elsa's* little bronze handle.

Elsa was a twenty-seven foot Calkins Bartender, as good a design as there is, and she proved to be a perfect boat for us. The Bartenders are still very much around, and while they sometimes get lost among more modern boats, they remain one of the saltiest, safest, and most attractive designs in the Northwest. Calkins designed them for the Coast Guard and they derive their name from their ability to navigate the treacherous river bars of the great rivers to the south of Juan de Fuca. They have the sea kindly characteristics of most double-enders and their planing boards enable them to achieve speeds of thirty knots.

Elsa was under-powered and would not plane, but she was still a dandy little boat. Down below--well, that's a bit of aggrandizement--in the forward V-berth there was a tiny wood stove called a "Little Pet." Doc Freeman in Seattle sold them back then before the EPA got in to the wood stove business. It was the size of a gallon paint can and burned little disks broken off Presto Logs. Sometimes, the Little Pet would get cherry red and the heat and the smell was really wonderful to us snuggled in a bedroll down in that little cave.

Otherwise, *Elsa's* outfitting was pretty much consistent with her windshield wiper. The depth sounder was a lead line, and while every boat should have one aboard, I don't think a string with knots in it and a lead sinker at the end ought to be the primary means of determining how deep the water is. The galley was an alcohol burner that would have been dangerous except that it was almost impossible to light and peak heat was somewhere below the boiling point of water. Never mind coffee between meals. There was a sink about the size of a soup bowl, and a little hand pump that sometimes supplied fresh water, but then only drop by precious drop. That was probably a good thing since there was not much fresh water to begin with. A hot bath happened if the little pump could fill a small pan and if the stove would work long enough to heat it and if we happened to be somewhere that the cockpit was shielded from view. Radio? You've got to be kidding.

Ward had circumnavigated Vancouver Island single-handed in *Elsa*, so we felt confident that she would take us to Kingcome

Inlet.

We had some charts, parallels, and dividers by this time, and a second-hand, nine channel VHF with a range of something like a mile and a half. We also had a background fear that we would at any moment fall off the edge of the earth. We drew lines on our charts, and checked off each island or marker as we passed. Through the San Juans, customs at Bedwell Harbour, the Gulf Islands, Dodd Narrows, Nanaimo, Georgia Strait, Pender Harbour, Malaspina Strait, Lund, Desolation Sound. On and on we went. I'm not sure how we made it through the Yuculta Rapids, but we did. Dent Rapids, Whirlpool Rapids, Devil's Elbow, Green Rapids, Blind Channel, Johnston Strait. We turned north and headed through a maze of islands toward our destination.

Leaving Simoom Sound, we rounded Bradley Point and entered a deep, quiet inlet. Ahead of us, near Philadelphia Point, five great landslides stretched from near the summit of Mt. Plowden to the waterline. It looked as if Ursa Major had ripped out the vegetation right down to the bare white granite skeleton of the earth. Beneath the foreboding landslides we turned east into the next reach of Kingcome Inlet.

The day closed in: no wind, the water flat calm, clouds so low they formed a roof only a few feet above our heads, a roof that reached from the unbroken heavy, green conifer vegetation on one side to the other side of the narrowing inlet. The water changed to milk as it filled with glacial flour. We were in a silent, haunting tunnel: solid green on both sides, white above and below, the only sound the quiet background hum of our engine. Although Kingcome Inlet is not long, our anxiety magnified time and it seemed to us that we traveled for hours. Eventually over on the left shore, somewhere beyond Charles Creek, the monochromatic green wall was broken by a small white dot. We headed over to inspect. It was a sign, carved in Kwakwaka'wakw style, with the names and dates of three young men. They had been born on different days, but they had died on the same day, scarcely a year ago. It only added to the gloom.

We continued deeper into the inlet. We had not seen another boat or person since we turned beneath the landslides and our apprehension and discomfort was intense. Finally we rounded Petley Point and found a floating dock chained to a sheer rock wall. We had read that there was a public dock at the head of the inlet, but could this be it? The dock did not look like a public facility. About forty feet long and ten feet wide, it held a small open shed and an accumulation of what looked like personal property and trash. There was nothing else around, so this must be the staging area for heading up the river to the village. There seemed to be no other options and it was late. We tied to the dock, hoping we were not violating private property. It was raining.

A series of enigmatic pictographs were on the vertical rock face not far from the dock. The old images, their ochre color still strong despite some graffiti overlay were of animals, sailing ships, and coppers.

We were way beyond our comfort level. I am not an especially intuitive person; rather, I tend to pick up on physical objects, concrete events, and rational contexts. But by this time my intuition had kicked in big time. I have never been anywhere I felt more unwelcome. And this was coming from the natural environment. We had not seen a soul. But we knew we were in foreign territory and we were pretty sure that we did not belong.

The day continued to weird out. Shortly before dinner time we saw a skiff approaching. A man, clearly not Native, rowed toward us. "Ya got a mickey?" he yelled when he got closer. I had no idea whether I had a "mickey" or not. A wrench? A beer? Finally we worked things out. He wanted a CB radio. He had been taking a small tugboat up the river and it was stuck on a sandbar up there somewhere. He wanted to radio the logging camp further upstream for help. When he learned that we did not have a "mickey" he asked us if we would take him in *Elsa* up the river to "the ranch" where there was a radio-telephone he could use. I knew from what I had read that the Halliday ranch was up there somewhere, but I thought it was abandoned. "No," he said, "there are people there." I was reluctant to take *Elsa* up the river. He had already stuck his own boat on a sand bar. Nevertheless, he insisted that he could get us safely up as far as "the ranch."

So we went. The river current against us was strong and our progress slow as we worked our way back and forth around the sand bars. However, within a couple of miles we found the dilapidated dock on the western bank of the river. We tied against the current although I wasn't sure the dock would hold. The Halliday ranch was famous as one of the first homesteads in the region. William and Ernest Halliday had first visited the Kingcome in 1893 and a year later staked homesteads and moved their families into rough cabins. Later they built substantial homes, cleared land and planted crops. It did not seem to occur to the Hallidays that the land was the traditional homeland of the people who lived at Gwa'yi, nor did it seem to occur to them that the native crab apples, clover, and silverweed they cleared for grazing land were essential parts of the native diet.

The Halliday Ranch had been famous for almost a hundred years and I expected something like Bonanza. What I found was more like Tobacco Road. We tramped through high grass and an unkempt yard to the house that looked like it would collapse before the dock did. The paint had long since peeled away, exposing the grey siding. The woman who answered the door matched the house. She was neither attractive nor friendly. She somewhat grudgingly let the tug boat skipper use the radio telephone. I opted to wait outside.

The call for help completed, we returned in *Elsa* to the relative security of the dock at the head of the Inlet. The tug boat skipper headed back up river in his skiff to await help from the camp and we settled in for the evening tied to the dock and next to the haunting pictographs. During the night we were awakened by an outboard and loud, unfriendly voices. We could not distinguish the words, but the cadence was Native, and it was clear that they were drunk. We were afraid we might be boarded, but the only assault was verbal and finally they left.

The next morning it was still raining. The strange feeling of not belonging remained; the sign marking the death of three men haunted us, as did the visit of drunks during the night. We were clearly beyond our comfort level and before breakfast we left too. After all those months of planning and weeks of travel and within four miles of our destination, we fled. Intuition and feelings had trumped curiosity and adventure.

Twenty-five years later I returned to Kingcome Inlet. During those years I made repeated trips to the Broughton Archipelago and while the village beyond the dock remained lodged in my memory and Kingcome Inlet was just beyond Bradley Point, I always stopped short of the great landslides that marked the Inlet itself.

In the Broughton's I especially liked Echo Bay and every year I would tie to the dock at Windsong Barge for a visit with Jim and

Muffin O'Donnell and their daughters, Cedar and Willow. Jim and Muffin had moved to the area during the hippy era and built a whimsical house on a barge. They developed a small marina and fishing camp and raised their daughters. Today Jim and Muffin (now Christine) are divorced and Windsong Barge has been sold. But in those earlier and perhaps more innocent days, I got to know Jim and Muffin a bit and looked forward to my yearly visit. I also found other friends in the area--Billy Proctor, Alexandra Morton, Paul and Helena Spong, Jim and Mary Bowerman, David Garrick, Bill and Donna McKay. I regularly visited Insect Island and Village Island, both steeped in ancient tradition and mystery. And I relished a stay at Kwatsi Bay and a visit with Max Knierim and Anka Fraser and the precocious and delightful younger members of the family, Marieke and Russell.

The journey to the Broughtons always included a stop in Refuge Cove, and one year next to the fishing tackle display in the small store I found a book by Judith Williams, Two Wolves at the Dawn of Time: Kingcome Inlet Pictographs, 1893-1998. By the time I finished Judith's book, I realized it was time for me to return to the Inlet. For the first time I learned that the name of the village is Gwa'yi, and just as Margaret Craven's I Heard the Owl Call My Name had launched me on my first attempt to visit Gwa'yi, Judith Williams' book touched off the second.

From Max and Anca at Kwatsi Bay I learned that Lorne Brown at Shawl Bay might be able to arrange a visit for us.

We went to Shawl Bay and talked with Lorne. He said he would see what he could do, but that sometimes radio contact with the village was difficult. That evening, we joined the traditional Shawl Bay dock party where the centerpiece was a blender powered by a gasoline engine: Margaritas on the docks--like no others.

The next morning Lorne said he had talked to Dave Dawson at Gwa'yi and that Dave would meet us at the government dock at the head of the Inlet at noon. This time, instead of twenty-seven foot *Elsa* with her little wood stove and lead-line, we were in *Shadow*. She was steel, fifty-two feet, two depth sounders, two radars, and 2000 gallons of diesel. But the landslides were still on the mountain as we turned into Kingcome Inlet, and the water was still filled with glacial flour. We tied to the dock where I had tied 25 years earlier.

The foreboding and anxiety that had dominated my first visit to this estuary and dock were no longer present. It was not only that I had more experience on the water and that my boat was bigger and sturdier. It was mainly that I knew it was OK for me to be here. I had been invited. It was not raining.

The Inlet, the estuary, the famous potlatch pictographs, and the dock all seemed to be pretty much as they had been twenty-five years earlier. Of course, while my memory was a quarter of a century old, the inlet and village had not remained frozen in time. Now on the sheer rock face high above the dock, a giant modern pictograph greated us. Its intense ochre images dominated the area.

We had learned from Judith Williams' book that the old pictographs were meant to call attention to a great potlatch attended by people from Gwa'yi that was held in 1921 in violation of the government's anti-potlatch law. William Halliday who had built the old grey house we had visited with the tugboat skipper, was the Indian Agent for that area, and had become notorious for his ruthless efforts to suppress the potlatch and centuries of vibrant Kwakwaka'wakw culture. The long abandoned residential school, evidence of these draconian policies, still stands in Alert Bay.

Halliday had jailed potlatch participants and had confiscated priceless ceremonial art work that was generations old. He sent what he considered the "best" of the ceremonial objects to various government museums, sold some to private collectors, and destroyed the rest of this magnificent traditional regalia. The anti-potlatch law and its ruthless enforcement had been a defining event for the Kwakwaka'wakw people. In spite of the best efforts of the settlers and the government however, the people of Gwayi survived. Fifty years later, in the 1970's, many of the confiscated ceremonial objects were repatriated to the U'Mista Cultural Center in Alert Bay. Now that Center is a major force in the life of this ancient culture.

From Judith's book we also learned about the new rock art. Marianne Nicolson, who had studied art at the University of Victoria, and for whom Gwa'yi was home, created the huge new pictograph in 1998. Not far from the traditional pictographs documenting the famous 1921 potlatch, Marianne had painted the first tribal pictograph in seventy years. It was big - over 35 feet high, and its execution was another major event in the area. For generations, and until as recently as 1955, a great greeting statue had stood near the mouth of the river., proclaiming the territory of the people of Gwa'yi. Where once the great statue had served as a welcoming sign and a greeting, now instead Marianne's pictograph proclaims the territory and people of Gwa'yi.

While some traditionalists argued that pictographs were a part of the past, Marianne thought it was important to document the vitality of her village, the people, and their traditions. Art, history and place merge in this new pictograph which welcomes us to Gwa'yi, just as the ancient statue had welcomed visitors for so many years.

Under this great painting, we waited for Dave to pick us up. About noon an outboard skiff arrived. It was not Dave, but his nephew, Clyde Dawson. Clyde made us feel welcome and soon we were in his skiff headed up the river where fear had turned us back 25 years before. But this time the helmsman knew the river. We dodged the sandbars, passed the still broken down dock at the old Halliday place, passed the grey Halliday house, and continued on to the village.

The Dzawada'enuxw people who live at Gwa'yi are one of the four Kwakwaka'wakw sub-groups. While native people were forced from other traditional sites by disease, missionaries and starvation and were relocated to towns and "reserves," the people who lived at Gwa'yi did not leave. Its location, four miles up a sand-bar clogged river has given it both isolation and extraordinary protection.

Gwa'yi is distinctive in other ways. For generations it has been famous throughout the Northwest and well in to the interior for its oolichan, a sardine sized, very oily fish. Gwa'yi's oolichan oil was a major trading commodity for centuries.

We left Clyde's outboard on the beach and he took us to meet his aunt and uncle, Dave and Ruth Dawson. Ruth served fresh cookies with coffee and we felt very welcomed and privileged to experience the warmth, hospitality, and informality of the people of Gwa'yi.

Time warped as we toured the village with Clyde. We stood in front of the old Anglican Church with its pulpit supported on the wings of an eagle and remembered Margaret Craven's book that had drawn us to this spot half a lifetime ago. And we remembered the priest in the story who had come here to minister and, who instead found himself ministered to by the integrity of the community and the way of life that had nurtured generation after generation on this bit of land and sea.

Then weaving into the present we toured a brand new school building and an equally new health center. For the first time people who live in Gwa'yi may utilize the benefits of European education and medicine without having to leave their traditional home. And some things never change. A man approached us trying to sell trading beads he had recently dug in the village. We finally bought a carved serving spoon.

We entered the shadows of the old big house. Ryan, a young man about eighteen years old, was practicing traditional songs to the beat of the drum log. We left the dark and smoky old building and were shown a new big house under construction. Nearby we met Willy Hawkins who was carving the posts and beams for the new big house, their colors and shapes reminiscent of the old house. On the beach, several other carvers were shaping the huge logs that will support the roof.

When we said goodbye to Dave and Ruth, they gave us a fresh Sockeye and three beautiful Dungeness crabs. Clyde brought his young son along when he returned us to the government dock, and we were accompanied by a group of young people with iPods. They were making their own way downstream to the dock to meet Bill McKay who would take them in his ultra-modern fast aluminum *Naiad Explorer* to Alert Bay for a traditional canoe race with First Nations canoes from throughout the coastal region. Here was a microcosm of the rare blending of past and present, white and native cultures, tradition and technology.

After *Naiad Explorer* left and Clyde and his son had returned up the river, we were alone again at the doorway to Gwa'yi where Marianne's new pictograph stands next to the ancient images, integrating art, place, and history."

As I write now, I reflect on the twenty-five years between my two visits to Kingcome Inlet and the countless centuries people have lived there in peace. I have come to a new appreciation of the richness, beauty, and depth of the great cultures of the indigenous people of the Northwest. I am beginning to understand the story of the two wolves, Kwalili and Kawadilikala, who were the fathers of the Dzawada'enuxw and Haxwa'mis people, who founded Gwa'yi and who gave birth to the first human beings at the beginning of time. Now I am beginning to understand the mystery and magic that attracted me to the Inside Passage thirty-three years ago and that has drawn me back again and again. It is the accessibility of nature and history lived in this place. From Kwalili and Kawadilikala to Ward Williams who built his boat, named her *Elsa* after his mother and sailed her single-handed around Vancouver Island, the place lets me get in touch with its local truth. The landslides scraped down Mt. Plowden at the head of Kingcome Inlet expose the granite of the earth and offer to expose the depth of my own soul.

As I worked on the final revision of this story, a friend handed me The Lure of the Local by Lucy R. Lippard. I read:

"The intersections of nature, culture, history, and ideology form the ground, on which we stand--our land, our place, the local. The lure of the local is the pull of place that operates on each of us, exposing our politics and our spiritual legacies. It is the geographical component of the psychological need to belong somewhere, one antidote to a prevailing alienation. The lure of the local is that undertone to modern life that connects it to the past we know so little and the future we are aimlessly concocting. It is not universal (nothing is) and its character and

affect differ greatly overtime from person to person and from community to community. For some people the lure of the local is neither felt nor acknowledged; for some it is an unattainable dream; for others it is a bittersweet reality, at once comforting and constricting; for others it is only partial reality, partial dream. These days the notion of the local is attractive to many who have never really experienced it, who may or may not be willing to take the responsibility and study the local knowledge that distinguishes every place from every other place."

Now I feel a part of the place—the whole of it—and the cultures that have shaped and been shaped by it. Earlier I wrote that going north, I cross a line and the animals are no longer in my world, but instead, I am in their world. Now there is this deeper sense of being part of nature, history, tradition, art, and culture. Here, it all fits together and I have come full circle. Like the priest in Margaret Craven's book, I now know that in exploring The Inside Passage to Alaska, I have begun to discover the inside passage to myself.

20 SPRINGER RETURNS HOME

D o whales and humans communicate? Ask Ahab. Humans
chased sperm whales in every ocean, slaughtering them for
their oil to light our lamps and their baleen to make our corsets. A
century later we kidnapped orca whales; put them in prisons we
call tourist attractions, and fed them fish for jumping through our
hoops. We communicate.

Fortunately, that's not the end of the story. In recent years
both the US and Canada, along with many other nations, have
changed their laws to protect orcas. Now efforts abound to nur-
ture these gentle creatures, and during an amazing week in July of
2002, we were pulled into a adventure beyond our wildest dreams
regarding a young orca.

When *Shadow* left Friday Harbor on July 1, 2002, we were
on our way through the Inside Passage to Alaska. A week later we
made one of our regular stops in Telegraph Cove near the northern end of Vancouver Island. We had no idea we were about to
begin a grand adventure.

Boaters heading north frequently pass by Telegraph Cove. The
small harbor provides no room for anchoring and the few docks

are crowded with small local boats. Pleasure boaters usually head a few miles north to Port McNeill where there are restaurants, stores, and ample moorage. Commercial boats tend to head a few miles further north to the larger town of Port Hardy.

During the economic boom of the last decade, developers attempted a major project in Telegraph Cove, but the subsequent economic downturn left their efforts half-finished and somewhat forlorn. Telegraph Cove remains a small quiet cove, a place where kayakers embark for paddles around the protected waters, and a few tourists board the classic tug, *Gikumi*, to search Johnston Strait hoping for a sighting of the orca whales that frequent the area.

Nevertheless, Telegraph Cove holds a particular attraction for me. Jim and Mary Bowerman, who own *Gikumi* and operate her through Orcella Expeditions, usually invite *Shadow* to side-tie next to *Gikumi*. The whale museum and gift shop created by Jim and Mary is always interesting. The ancient Atlas diesel engine from my old boat *Sundown* has been resurrected from some dead engine graveyard and given a new coat of green paint. With her brass parts polished and looking like she might even run, she is now the centerpiece in the foyer of the quaint little restaurant on the dock.

Today, however, *Gikumi* was out in the Straits, so we shoe-horned ourselves into one of the few tight spaces available for visitors. Once *Shadow* was secure, I walked the docks, looking and listening. Something was going on. The docks were crowded and there was a palpable feeling of energy and excitement in the air.

We had arrived in the middle of an international media event! TV vans, with their satellite antennas, ringed the shore. An orphaned orca whale nicknamed Springer and lost for months a hundred miles south in Puget Sound, was about to be returned to her home waters here. We had arrived one day ahead of her expected return.

Springer had been found the previous winter near Seattle, far from her home waters and whale family. She was sick, under-nourished, and lonesome. With no other whales in south Puget Sound, Springer had tried to make friends with local boats. Her search for companionship had even resulted in delays for the state ferries that ply the south sound's waters.

Springer's predicament had attracted so much attention because orca whales living in the Pacific Northwest were already well known. Until the mid- 1900's, relatively little was known about orcas, sometimes called killer whales and sometimes blackfish. Prior to about 1950 it was thought that orcas were destructive and even dangerous. They were shot by fishermen who thought they ate too many salmon and the governments of the US and Canada paid bounties for their slaughter. Between 1962 and 1973 at least fifty orcas were brutally captured for display in marine aquaria. Some were killed in the process.

Shortly after 1970 things began to change. A marine biologist, Michael Bigg, developed an intense passion for killer whales and revolutionized our knowledge of them. Bigg discovered that the orca population in the northwest was approximately 350 individuals. Previously it had been thought they numbered in the thousands. Bigg found that individual orcas could be identified by distinctive markings on their dorsal fins and saddle patches. He also realized that individual whales could be identified by their distinctive vocalizations. Through the efforts of hundreds of observers and thousands of pictures, he organized a huge effort to identify individual whales. Bigg's method and nomenclature for identifying orcas is still in use. He discovered that orcas are highly matrilineal, living in tightly organized pods of ten to fifty individuals. He labeled these pods alphabetically, A, B, C, etc., and numbered individuals within each pod. Bigg realized that there were two groups of orca pods in the Pacific Northwest, the southern residents around the San Juan Islands in the United States, and the northern residents around Johnston Strait in Canada. Springer was known, therefore as A73, and identified as belonging to the northern resident group.

After Springer had been identified, a protracted debate among professionals and in the media emerged over what should be done. Her present situation and future became a national media event. Some people felt she should be left alone letting "nature" take its course. Others felt she should be captured and sent to an aquarium. Finally, it was decided Springer should be gently captured, restored to health, and released in her home waters. Although there were no precedents for this process, it worked. After six months of professional care, Springer was ready for release in her Canadian home waters. This young orca, now an international celebrity, was expected to arrive the next day from Seattle. She would be traveling aboard a donated 140 foot catamaran. It was an experiment that had never before been attempted.

Springer's expected arrival the next day created the excitement we had found in Telegraph Cove that July afternoon. In a serendipitous turn of events, we morphed from observer to participant. The boat intended as an observation platform next to Springer's holding pen had proved unusable. Somewhat desperate representatives from the Vancouver Aquarium asked us if *Shadow* could be used as an observation platform during Springer's acclimatization. *Shadow* would be tied to Springer's pen for observers keeping twenty-four hour watch. We were warned we might be obligated for as long as two or three weeks until Springer's home pod returned.

It sounded like an adventure. We had to shift from our relaxed cruising pace to the fast-moving world of whale experts and media.

Springer would arrive the following day. *Shadow* had to be in place immediately. With the help of aquarium personnel we reoriented ourselves and reorganized *Shadow*. We moved from the excitement of Telegraph Cove to a secluded bay on Hanson Island. We tied to the fish-farm net pens prepared for Springer and waited for whatever would happen next. *Shadow* was the only boat permitted inside an exclusion zone, protected by the Canadian Coast Guard and the RCMP.

Springer arrived the next afternoon as planned. Her fast catamaran made the trip in ten hours. It had taken us a week. She was greeted by a phenomenal array of marine biologists, representatives of the US Coast Guard, US Customs, National Marine Fisheries, Canadian Customs, Canadian Coast Guard, the RCMP, Canadian Department of Fisheries and Oceans, US and Canadian Veterinarians, Whale Experts, Whale Watchers, First Nations representatives, media boats and others. Springer was hoisted from her catamaran onto the deck of a crane barge and, with great care from her handlers and animal health experts, brought to her temporary new home.

The only person not there, conspicuous by her absence, was Alexandra Morton, a noted authority on the northern residents. Alexandra lives nearby and has devoted her life to the protection of the northern resident orcas. Alexandra has also been a visible and effective opponent of fish farms because of their disastrous impact on the environment and on native salmon runs. Consequently, as a condition for the use of their net pens, Stoldt Seafood, owner of many fish farms in the area, had specified that Alexandra be excluded. That one act proved the defensiveness of the fish farms and the effectiveness of Alexandra's work.

Shortly before Springer arrived, Chief Bill Cranmer from Alert Bay and other elders representing First Nations arrived aboard *Shadow* to constitute a welcoming party. The chiefs had arrived in magnificent canoes with many paddlers in ceremonial clothing. Six native purse seiners had anchored off the cove and native people, many in traditional clothing, lined the shores. While those of us reared in western civilization may wonder if humans and whales communicate, it is not a question for tribal people.

Springer lay quietly in her sling on the barge as it maneuvered to the net pen. Then, as her caregivers hovered about, she was given a final round of medical tests. Hoisted slowly up and over, she was gently lowered into the pen to be received by a team of divers led by Jeff Foster from Ocean Futures. Once out of the sling, Springer took command. She spy-hopped, breeched, jumped, tail splashed, flipper slapped, and generally cavorted like a killer whale. Assisted by intense native drummers, Chief Cranmer conducted an impressive traditional welcoming ceremony.

The bay began to empty quickly. Her handlers intended that Springer receive minimum human contact once she had arrived safely. Well before dark, a few remaining observers were aboard *Shadow* and we relaxed in the saloon and rehashed the day's excitement and potential perils. Congratulations and thanks were exchanged regarding the glories of the day and we discussed the possibility of waiting weeks for Springer's family to appear.

After we turned in, with the hydrophone, we heard Springer continuing to vocalize through the night. Her entire pen was lit by phosphorescence as she swam calmly and gently.

The next morning, Springer was much more active and restless. In a totally unexpected turn of events, Springer's home pod had appeared in the area! Although the experts had thought it might take weeks for the pod to realize that Springer was near, her closest relatives had arrived within a day. There was tremendous excitement everywhere.

It seemed almost unbelievable that members of her home pod would arrive so quickly, but there they were, out in Blackfish Sound. Paul Spong and Helena Symond from OrcaLab were monitoring the movement of A Pod through hydrophones located throughout the area. Away from the net pens, Alexandra Morton was back at work on the water monitoring the whales from her small sturdy boat, *Blackfish Sound*. Kim and Scott from Straitwatch, as well as others, were also maintaining an on-the-water watch. The pod had begun to move toward us.

While the pod approached, tension built around the pen and aboard *Shadow*. No one was quite ready for events to develop so quickly. A mad scramble ensued as the command was given to prepare for a possible release. Jeanine Siemens and her team from Stoldt Fisheries began to shorten the nets. Clint Wright and his crew from the Vancouver Aquarium donned dry suits and splashed into Springer's pen. While all the humans were bustling about, Springer remained contrastingly calm. She gently allowed herself to be eased into the now shallow nets and lay quietly as GPS transmitters were attached with suction cups just below her dorsal fin. John Ford, Graham Ellis and Lance Barrett-Lennard, the biological team, were in boats in the strait monitoring the movements of the pod. Pete Schroeder, the veterinarian who had monitored Springer's health since she arrived in Puget Sound months ago, was on the walkway as if he were a parent seeing his first born leaving home for college.

Finally, after seemingly endless radio discussions and delays, the decision came: Drop the nets! Ever so quickly, this small mammal that had been the object of such intense care by so many people was gone! Cheers erupted from throughout the bay; wild applause was everywhere. It must have been a bittersweet moment for many people who had devoted so much energy to her well-being.

Through the night Graham Ellis, John Ford, and the team from OrcaLab monitored Springer's position with hydrophones. By morning we were receiving moment-by-moment reports from Alexandra Morton, who was now very much a part of the picture. It was not clear whether Springer was uniting with her pod. The hydrophones and GPS transmitters told us that Springer was in the general vicinity of her pod, although the distance between them seemed to be growing. Perhaps, after months of failing health and captivity, she was still just a little too weak to keep up. Or maybe there was some other dynamic at work.

The next 48 hours were intense. Springer was tracked by Graham Ellis in *Shamis*, Helena and Paul at OrcaLab, Nic and Scott from Strait Watch, the folks from Stubbs Island Tours, Bill McKay on *Naiad Explorer*, and many others. Hourly her behavior sent everyone involved from elation to concern. Once again she attempted to befriend boats, circling and bumping some hapless sport fishing boat. With help from Springer's observers, the alarmed fishermen were extricated. There was an exceptionally large number of killer whales in the area and from time to time

Springer appeared to be integrated, or at least within proximity. At other times she seemed as lost as she had been in Puget Sound.

The next three days were days of constant tracking and monitoring. We took advantage of some slack time to visit U'Mista, the native museum in Alert Bay, with its remarkable collection of First Nations masks and artifacts housed in a traditional long house style building. The museum is a testament to the ability of tribal culture to survive the best efforts of Western European civilization to obliterate it and steal its land, heritage, and power.

Two nights later, as we were eating dinner aboard *Shadow*, safely anchored in a quiet cove on nearby Village Island, tribal representatives approached with drumming and singing. We were invited to visit the ancient village site, Mimkwumlis (Mamalilaculla), for a killer whale dance welcoming the return of one of their own. Pete Schroeder, in a gesture typical of his amazing sensitivity, presented the tribal representatives with Springer's stick, a four-foot Alder log she had adopted in Puget Sound and that had accompanied her throughout her odyssey as her security blanket.

A few days later we left Telegraph Cove and Blackfish Sound not knowing whether Springer would join her pod and not knowing if she would survive the winter. We continued to make our way north through the Inside Passage to Alaska, leaving Springer, her relatives, and her human observers.

Two years later we returned to Telegraph Cove. We had received reports that Springer was thriving. She had returned two years running with her pod. Pete Schroeder wanted to see her with her pod for himself, so we again headed north in *Shadow*. When we arrived in Telegraph Cove, we were invited aboard *Naiad Explorer*, Bill MacKay's beautiful and efficient whale watching boat, and spent a marvelous day with Springer and her pod.

The next morning we were headed south. In spite of the thick fog covering the area, we were hungry for one more visit with Springer. In the middle of the channel, in the middle of the fog, we radioed Bill MacKay for information about where to find Springer and her pod. "Just stop were you are, Joseph," he replied. "They are headed your way." We stopped the engine and gathered on the side deck, straining to see through the fog. Then the entire A pod of twenty or thirty whales appeared. As they approached *Shadow*, the A pod formed a line facing us. Each spring when the pods return to their summer feeding grounds, they frequently great each other in this line formation. Springer was near the middle of the line. And then we were awed. The pod swam under the boat and Springer swam directly under Pete. We said not a word, but moved to the other side of the boat to watch the pod leave. About fifty yards out, they turned and again, forming a line, swam toward *Shadow*. And again, Springer swam directly under Pete.

Once again, the magic of the Inside Passage had opened my eyes and my heart to a realm of greater mystery. Satisfied that we now knew who was communicating with whom, we started the engine and, through the fog, headed south.

Inside Passage Distances: Seattle To Glacier Bay

	Miles	Total
Seattle to Friday Harbor	81	
Friday Harbor to Genoa Bay	34	115
Genoa Bay to Nanaimo	36	151
Nanaimo to Lund	75	226
Lund to Eveleigh Anchorage	15	241
Eveleigh Anchorage to the Yucultas	27	268
The Yucultas to Forward Harbour	28	296
Forward Harbour to Alert Bay	48	344
Alert Bay to Wells Passage	24	368
Wells Passage to Cape Caution	51	419
Cape Caution to Penrose Island	20	439
Penrose Island to Pruth Anchorage	21	460
Pruth Anchorage to Koeye River	12	472
Koeye River to Lizzie Cove	23	495

	Miles	Total
Lizzie Cove to Bella Bella	8	503
Bella Bella to Cougar Bay*	47	550
Cougar Bay* to Lowe Inlet	83	633
Lowe Inlet to Prince Rupert	60	693
Prince Rupert to Brundige Inlet	33	726
Brundige Inlet to Foggy Bay	27	753
Foggy Bay to Ketchikan	35	788
Ketchikan to Meyers Chuck	35	823
Meyers Chuck to Anan Creek	50	873
Anan Creek to Wrangell	15	888
Wrangell to Portage Bay	63	951
Portage Bay to Baranof Warm Springs	55	1006
Baranof Warm Springs to Sitka	84	1090
Sitka to Kimshan Cove	57	1147
Kimshan Cove to Elfin Cove	61	1208
Elfin Cove to Bartlett Cove	30	1238
Bartlett Cove to Reid Inlet	33	1271

*In 2015, when we turned into Cougar Bay, one of our favorite quiet anchorages, we found that clear cut logging had destroyed its serene beauty. Right down to the shoreline the land had been scraped bare of cedars and firs, the slopes leveled for an industrial wasteland of chain saws, trucks, trailers, generators, loaders and yarders. Brutal noise replaced the calls of ravens and loons. Throughout the Inside Passage chaos and destruction continue and accelerate.

ABOUT THE AUTHOR

I grew up in Texas, attended graduate school at Princeton University in New Jersey, and taught World Religions at the Universities of Alabama, Nebraska, and Western Washington.

When I moved to the Pacific Northwest my life took a new direction. The magic of the Northwest wilderness hooked me and I began to learn. I began to explore the Inside Passage to Alaska.

I returned repeatedly to the magical waterways and islands of Washington, British Columbia and Alaska, and for the first time in my life I knew I was home. A new world opened for me: maritime skills of piloting and navigation, history of the Northwest, native cultures, environmental degradation and protection, salmon, eagles, bears, whales, and wolves.

Eventually I abandoned the comfortable life of a tenured professor and moved to a small island north of Seattle. I started a charter business, with my classic northwest boat, *Sundown*, into the country I had come to love.

Inside The Inside Passage is not a story about a trip I took only once. I'm not a professional writer looking for something to write. I did this. I went there. I will go again. I learned and explored and messed around and then 20 years later I discovered that I had some stories to tell. This is the real thing; not a place I only visited.

About The Book Designer

I met Joseph at my adopted home in the Pacific Northwest. I had come a long way from my childhood in East Berlin. After escaping from Communist East Germany before the Wall came down, I studied in West Berlin, Ireland and Canada. Then after traveling through Europe, North America, Australia, Asia and South America I arrived "home" in the Okanogan Highlands, a remote and scenic area just east of the Cascade Mountains. Now I live here in a little wooden cabin amid mountain vistas and work as a full time artist.

I never gave up my passion for travel and discovery and when the opportunity to travel the Inside Passage to Alaska on *Orina* with Joseph presented itself I was ecstatic and said yes. I got to see many places and meet many people Joseph writes about in this book. The Inside Passage is a magic place. It unleashed much creativity in me and part of it manifested itself in the design of this book.

I did the oil pastel painting for the cover while passing through the rainy, foggy Grenville Channel. I took all the photos along the way, drew the maps and finally put Joseph's writing and my visuals together into this book.

I hope you enjoy reading it as much as I did.